# The history of marriage equality in Ireland

MANCHESTER
1824

Manchester University Press

# The history of marriage equality in Ireland

## A social revolution begins

SONJA TIERNAN

Manchester University Press

Published by Manchester University Press
Oxford Road, Manchester M13 9PL
www.manchesteruniversitypress.co.uk

British Library Cataloguing-in-Publication Data
A catalogue record for this book is available from the British Library

ISBN 978 1 5261 4599 4 hardback
ISBN 978 1 5261 6078 2 paperback

First published 2020

The publisher has no responsibility for the persistence or accuracy of URLs for any external or third-party internet websites referred to in this book, and does not guarantee that any content on such websites is, or will remain, accurate or appropriate.

Typeset by
Servis Filmsetting Ltd, Stockport, Cheshire

For Charlotte Hall Tiernan with love

We took on the job of levelling the playing pitch, and made it playable, if not entirely level. But there's still a game to be played.

Christopher Robson (1941–2013)

# Contents

# Acknowledgements

My thanks to Denise Charlton and Moninne Griffith who initially invited me to write the history of the campaign for marriage equality in Ireland. This book is ultimately their idea. My thanks to all those who worked towards the momentous victory of achieving civil marriage for same-sex couples in Ireland. Most especially thank you to Gráinne Healy, Andrew Hyland, Katherine Zappone and Ann Louise Gilligan who all took time out of their busy schedules to talk to me and help me piece together this history. Thank you also for an establishment fund granted from Yes Equality to ensure that this project was completed.

A sincere thank you to those people who kindly granted me copyright permission to publish large sections, or in some cases complete versions, of their related writings or speeches during and after the marriage equality referendum: Rory O'Neill (Panti Bliss) for permission to publish his Noble Call speech at the Abbey Theatre; Ursula Halligan for permission to republish her article 'Referendum led me to tell truth about myself,' originally published in the *Irish Times*; Archbishop Eamon Martin, Archbishop of Armagh, Apostolic Administrator of Dromore and Primate of All Ireland, for permission to republish his message on the marriage referendum, 'Care for the covenant of marriage'. I am grateful also to have been awarded a Moore Institute Visiting Fellowship at the National University of Ireland Galway in 2019 which gave me access to a wealth of archival and library resources to complete the final stages of writing this book. Many thanks to my colleague Liam McIlvanney for his unwavering support of my research and to Emer Lyons for compiling the index to this book and for her general positive impact on Irish Studies at the University of Otago.

As always thank you to my family and friends who never fail to support and encourage my work, especially Charlotte Hall Tiernan for proof reading the final manuscript in such fine detail. Finally, thank you to Ivana Bacik, who played an intrinsic role in the marriage equality campaign in Ireland from the earliest stages, for endorsing this book by writing the foreword.

# Marriage equality across the globe[1]

### The Netherlands (2001)

The Netherlands was the first country to legally introduce marriage equality, with an overwhelming majority vote in Parliament of 107–33 in favour.

### Belgium (2003)

Ninety-one Members of Parliament voted in favour of equal marriage, with only twenty-two votes against its introduction. Initially the new marriage bill excluded adoption rights for same-sex couples; this was adjusted in 2006.

### Spain (2005)

On 30 June 2005, the Spanish Parliament voted to end all restrictions excluding same-sex couples from marriage, with a vote of 187 to 147. The Spanish government under Prime Minister José Luis Rodíguez Zapatero simply added one line to existing legislation ensuring total equality with heterosexual unions: 'Marriage will have the same requirements and results when the two people entering into the contract are of the same sex or of different sexes.'

### Canada (2005)

The Civil Marriage Act was first read in Canada's House of Commons on 1 February. The act redefined civil marriage with a gender-neutral definition as 'the lawful union of two persons to the exclusion of all others'.[2] The act was passed in the House of Commons by a vote of 158–133 and was later cleared through Senate by a majority of 47 to

21. The Civil Marriage Act came into effect with Royal Assent on 20 July 2005.

## South Africa (2006)
In December 2005, a case was brought by the Lesbian and Gay Equality Project to the Constitutional Court of South Africa that the Marriage Act 'unconstitutionally excludes same-sex couples'.[3] The court decided that this exclusion violated the constitutional rights of individuals and ordered Parliament to address the injustice within twelve months. In November 2006, by 230 votes to 41, Parliament voted in favour of amending the Constitution and introducing equal marriage.

## Norway (2009)
On 27 June 2008, a new section under 'gender' was included in the Marriage Act, stating that 'two persons of opposite sex or of the same sex may contract marriage'. This amendment came into force on 1 January 2009, ending discrimination against same-sex couples marrying.[4]

## Portugal (2010)
A law was ratified by President Aníbal Cavaco Silva on 17 May 2010 extending marriage to same-sex couples. The original bill was introduced by Prime Minister José Sócrates in December 2009 and came into effect on 5 June 2010.

## Iceland (2010)
The Parliament of Iceland voted unanimously to include the words 'man and man, woman and woman' to the country's marriage laws. The vote was forty-nine in favour, with no member of parliament voting against.

## Argentina (2010)
Argentina became the first Latin American country to extend civil marriage to same-sex couples when the National Congress voted 33 to 27 in favour of the motion. President Cristina Fernández de Kirchner signed this into law on 21 July 2010.

## Denmark (2012)
In 1989, Denmark became the first country to introduce civil partnerships for same-sex couples. It took the country until 15 June 2012

to extend marriage to same-sex couples, with a vote of 85 to 24 in Parliament.

### Brazil (2013)
Freedom to Marry describe the situation in Brazil as 'somewhat confusing'[5] until 16 May 2013, when a National Justice Council decision ordered every state across Brazil to allow same-sex couples access to marriage.

### France (2013)
A bill to introduce marriage for same-sex couples became law on 18 May 2013 after support from both houses of Parliament.

### Uruguay (2013)
A law came into force on 5 August 2013, two days after President José Mujica signed a bill extending civil marriage to same-sex couples.

### New Zealand (2013)
The marriage bill passed through Parliament on 17 April 2013 and came into effect on 19 August that year.

### England and Wales (2014)
A law extending civil marriage to same-sex couples came into effect in England and Wales on 29 March 2014. The bill was debated numerous times in the House of Commons and in the House of Lords before receiving Royal Assent from Queen Elizabeth II on 17 July 2013.

### Scotland (2014)
An overwhelming majority of Members of the Scottish Parliament voted in support of legalising marriage for same-sex couples. The law came into effect on 16 December 2014.

### Luxembourg (2015)
In 2014, Luxembourg recognised a need to rewrite its antiquated marriage laws, which had not been subjected to major examination since 1804. The country's Prime Minister, Xavier Bettel, an openly gay man, put forward a bill to include full civil marriage equality. The bill was supported by Parliament by a vast majority of votes (56–4)

in the Chamber of Deputies. Marriage equality came into force on 1 January 2015.[6]

### Ireland (2015)

Marriage equality was passed by referendum vote of the people on 22 May 2015, signed into law by President Michael D. Higgins on 29 August and came into effect on 16 November 2015.

### Mexico – partial (2015)

On 3 June 2015, the Supreme Court of Mexico ruled that judges must grant injunctions to allow same-sex couples to marry in all thirty-one Mexican states. Some states have introduced laws extending marriage to same-sex couples without the need for injunctions. However, there is still work to be done by Lesbian, Gay, Bisexual and Transgender (LGBT) organisations to ensure that same-sex couples can access marriage equally in all states.

### The United States (2015)

On 26 June 2015, the Supreme Court ruled in favour of extending civil marriage to same-sex couples across all states of America.

### Greenland (2016)

Members of Parliament in Greenland voted in favour of adopting Denmark's marriage law, thus extending marriage to same-sex couples from 1 April 2016.

### Columbia (2016)

The highest court in Columbia, the Constitutional Court, ruled on 7 April 2016 to extend marriage to all. Marriage equality has been legal in Columbia since 28 April that year.

### Finland (2017)

In December 2014, Parliament voted 105 to 92 to legalise marriage for same-sex couples, the law being signed for approval by President Sauli Niinistö. It did not come into effect until 1 March 2017.

### Faroe Islands (2017)

On 1 July 2017, the Faroe Islands adopted the marriage law of Denmark, extending marriage to same-sex couples.

## Malta (2017)
Signed into law by President Coleiro Preca on 1 August 2017, marriage equality was legalised on 1 September the same year.

## Germany (2017)
On 20 July 2017, President Steinmeier signed the marriage bill extending marriage to same-sex couples in Germany despite initial objections from Chancellor Angela Merkel. The bill became legal on 1 October 2017.

## Australia (2017)
An unusual process was followed in Australia. Citizens took part in a postal vote on the issue of extending marriage to same-sex couples. The vote saw a 62 per cent majority in favour of extending marriage equality to same-sex couples but this was simply an opinion poll and had no legal basis through which the law could be changed. The positive response of the postal vote led the way for the Prime Minister Malcolm Turnbull to introduce a bill for a free vote in Parliament. The bill was passed and the law came into effect on 9 December 2017, with the first recorded marriage for a same-sex couple.

## Jersey (2018)
Although a Crown dependency within the UK, Jersey only extended marriage to same-sex couples in 2018. A bill was passed on 1 February and signed with Royal Assent on 23 May 2018.

## Austria (2019)
A Constitutional Court ruled that marriage would be legal for same-sex couples from 1 January 2019.

## Taiwan (2019)
On 24 May 2017, a Constitutional Court ruling concluded that same-sex couples should have the right to marry. The court ruled that laws should be enacted within two years of this date to extend civil marriage to same-sex couples. As on 21 February 2019 a draft bill was introduced which became legal on 24 May 2019.

## Costa Rica
The issue of marriage for same-sex couples reached the Supreme Court in Costa Rica, and on 8 August 2018 it declared that laws

prohibiting marriage for same-sex couples were unconstitutional. The court set a time period of eighteen months in which to enact laws extending civil marriage to same-sex couples. According to this ruling same-sex couples in Costa Rica will have access to marriage from 26 May 2020.

## Notes

1 Details in this table supported by research from David Masci, Elizabeth Sciupac and Michael Lipka, *Gay Marriage around the World*, Washington, September 2014; and 'The Freedom to Marry Internationally', Freedom to Marry USA website, available at: www.freedomtomarry.org/pages/the-freedom-to-marry-internationally (accessed 9 July 2018).

2 Mary C. Hurley, *Bill C-38: The Civil Marriage Act Canada*, Law and Government Division: 2 February 2005.

3 *Lesbian and Gay Equality Project and Eighteen Others v Minister of Home Affairs and Others*, in the Constitutional Court of South Africa, Southern African Legal Information Institute, 1 December 2005.

4 Ministry of Children and Equality, Norway, *The Marriage Act*, ACT 1991–07–04 No. 47.

5 'The Freedom to Marry Internationally'.

6 'Luxembourg legislature votes to legalize same-sex marriage, adoption', *LGBT Nation* (18 June 2014).

# Chronology of key events surrounding the Irish marriage equality campaign[1]

1993   Antiquated criminal law relating to homosexuality abolished (7 July)

Protection for lesbian and gay workers enshrined in updated Unfair Dismissals Act (14 July)

1996   Refugee Act includes protection from persecution on grounds of sexual orientation (26 June)

1998   Employment Equality Act protects lesbian and gay workers regarding recruitment and employment (18 June)

1999   Equality Authority established (18 October)

2000   Equal Status Act introduced – protects people against discrimination in the provision of goods and services on nine grounds, including sexual orientation (26 April)

2003   Ann Louise Gilligan and Katherine Zappone marry in Canadian Province of British Columbia (13 September)

2004   Civil Registration Act updated; now includes declaration prohibiting marriage between two people of the same sex (27 February)

KAL (an acronym of the first names of Katherine Zappone and Ann Louise Gilligan) challenge to Revenue Commission granted by Mr Justice Liam McKechnie at the High Court (8 November)

Senator David Norris introduces a Private Members, Civil Partnership, bill in the Seanad (9 December)

2005   Revenue Commissioners and the State file defence to KAL case (May)

Civil partnership introduced in UK, including Northern Ireland (19 December)

2006    Equality Authority states legal requirement under Belfast
        Agreement to provide same rights in Republic as in
        Northern Ireland (January)
        Bertie Ahern TD is the first Taoiseach to officially attend a
        lesbian and gay event – the opening of the Gay and Lesbian
        Equality Network's (GLEN's) new offices (3 April)
        Irish Council for Civil Liberties report, *Equality for All
        Families* (April)
        Hearing of Zappone & Gilligan High Court case (3–13
        October)
        Government Working Group on Domestic Partnership,
        'Colley Report', identifies marriage as the only full equality
        option for same-sex couples (November)
        Publication of Labour Party Civil Unions Bill using model
        suggested by Colley group (December)
2007    Labour Party Civil Unions Bill defeated (20 February)
        New coalition government, Fianna Fáil and Green Party,
        formed in June, commits to civil partnership based on
        Colley group findings (13 June)
        First expert meeting on the recognition of married same-sex
        couples at European Parliament (November)
2008    Marriage Equality established (February)
        The Department of Justice, Equality and Law Reform pub-
        lishes a draft proposal entitled 'General Scheme of Civil
        Partnership Bill' (June).[2]
2009    Presentation of full Civil Partnership Bill (26 June)
        Civil Partnership Bill introduced and debated in Oireachtas
        (December 2009/January 2010)
2010    Forty-seven European countries, including Ireland, agree on
        measures to combat discrimination on grounds of sexual
        orientation or gender identity (March)
        The Civil Partnership and Certain Rights and Obligations of
        Cohabitants Act 2010 passes with support of all parties;
        President Mary McAleese signs it into law (July)
        Social Welfare Act updated to include provision for civil
        partners to be treated equally to married couples (December)
        Law Reform Commission recommends extension of
        guardianship rights to children of civil partners (21
        December)

2011   Civil Partnership Act comes into effect on New Year's Day in Ireland (1 January)

New Programme for Government to address omissions from Civil Partnership Act relating to children and certain tax aspects (6 March)

New coalition government formed, Fine Gael and Labour (9 March)

First public civil partnership takes place – positive reception across national media (5 April)

Finance (No. 3) Act introduced by Minister for Finance, Michael Noonan, providing civil partners the same provisions as married couples for tax purposes (June)

Minister for Justice, Alan Shatter, amends citizenship provisions to provide equality for civil partners (July)

Minister Shatter signs an order recognising foreign same-sex registered relationships as Irish civil partnerships (December)

2012   Main political parties – Fianna Fáil, Labour, Sinn Féin and the Greens – support moves towards marriage for same-sex couples

Motion passed at Fine Gael Ard Fheis to prioritise marriage equality in Constitutional Convention (31 March)

Employment Equality (Amendment) Bill proposed by Averil Power to protect LGBT employees in religious-run institutions (February; defeated May)

Cian O'Callaghan, elected as mayor of Fingal County Council, Ireland's first openly gay mayor (June)

Cork City Council votes unanimously to support civil marriage for same-sex couples, closely followed by other local authorities around the Republic (July)

Minister for Justice, Alan Shatter, announces he will introduce bill with parenting reforms for lesbian and gay families (November)

Tánaiste, Eamon Gilmore, calls for referendum on marriage equality (13 November)

Chief Justice of Ireland, Mrs Justice Susan Denham, launches guides to civil partnership in the Four Courts (20 December)

Constitutional Convention formally established: a forum of one hundred people tasked with examining numerous aspects of the Irish Constitution, including marriage equality (1 December)

2013  Constitutional Convention calls for legal changes to ensure equal status for same-sex couples and their families – suggests referendum on the issue of equal access to civil marriage (24 April)

Department of Justice and Equality publishes briefing note on Family Relationships and Children Bill 2013, aiming to create a legal structure and provide clarity on parental rights and duties in diverse family forms (November)

Convention recommendations accepted and government announces a proposed referendum in Spring 2015 (17 December)

2015  Introduction of Children and Family Relationship Act 2015 (12 March)

Referendum to extend marriage to same-sex couples (22 May 2015)

2018  Children and Family Relationship (Amendment) Act 2018 passes both Houses of the Oireachtas to rectify errors with original bill (18 July)

2019  Civil Registration Bill (2019) passed allowing both parents in a female same-sex relationship to be entered on their child's birth certificate (15 May)

Northern Ireland (Executive Formation etc) Act 2019 passed. Northern Ireland Assembly did not reconvene before 21 October 2019, marriage extended to same-sex couples from 13 January 2020 (24 July)

## Notes

1 From amalgamated sources including Íde O'Carroll and Finbar McDonnell, *Marriage Equality: Case study, final version* (September 2010); and *GLEN briefing note on equal access to civil marriage* (2013), available at: www.glen.ie/attachments/GLEN_Briefing_Note_on_Equal_Access_to_Civil_Marriage.pdf (accessed 9 July 2018).

2 The report is available on the Department of Justice, Equality and Law Reform archive site: https://web.archive.org/web/20100110083414/http://www.justice.ie/en/JELR/Pages/General_Scheme_of_Civil_Partnership_Bill (accessed 20 August 2019).

# Foreword

*Ivana Bacik*

In May 2015, Ireland became the first country in the world to legalise marriage for gay couples through popular vote. The marriage equality referendum, passed by a 62 per cent majority, made international headlines. LGBT activists and groups all over the world have since sought to learn from the success of Ireland's social movement, the Yes Equality campaign, that achieved such historic progress in this traditionally conservative and Catholic country. This book will provide readers with clear insights into the campaign itself, and cogent analysis as to how the victory was won. Sonja Tiernan's invaluable contribution to the history of social progress in Ireland recognises and celebrates the many unsung heroes who worked for long years to achieve the historic 2015 result. She also ensures that the challenges and lessons of the campaign are documented, so that others may learn about how hearts and minds can be changed. Now, in the aftermath of a further successful referendum campaign in May 2018, this time to repeal the Eighth Amendment to the Constitution and ensure women's access to legal abortion in Ireland, another giant leap forward for progressive social change has been made. During the 2018 debates on women's reproductive health, many parallels were drawn with the marriage equality strategies; it became clear that we had learned much from the success of the Yes Equality campaign.

This book details the development of that campaign, from decriminalisation of homosexuality in 1993, to the initial litigation on marriage equality, to the legalisation of civil partnership, the establishment of the Constitutional Convention, and the referendum campaign itself. I feel privileged to have played some role in these events. As a practising barrister, I was Junior Counsel for Katherine

Zappone (now Minister for Children and Youth Affairs) and Ann
Louise Gilligan, now sadly passed away, in their ground-breaking
case seeking recognition of marriage equality (the KAL case); as an
activist and later as a Senator, over many years I campaigned and
agitated for greater LGBT rights and for legalisation of same-sex
marriage. But over all those years, even as we came close to winning
the referendum, it was hard for many of us to believe that we could
win; that we could achieve such a resounding result for equality, given
Ireland's historically poor record on gay rights.

In reality, over the decades prior to 2015 Ireland had moved very
slowly towards equal treatment for the LGBT community. The provisions of the 1861 Offences Against the Person Act criminalising
homosexuality had remained in force in Ireland many years after
their repeal in England under the Sexual Offences Act 1967. By the
late 1970s, a campaign was underway to seek their repeal in Ireland;
it was spearheaded by David Norris, later to become a Senator. In
1977 he initiated a legal challenge to the constitutionality of the
legal provisions of the 1861 act which criminalised sexual activity
between men. He lost his case in the High Court and appealed to the
Supreme Court, where he lost again in 1983. The majority judgment
there was given by then Chief Justice O'Higgins, in an infamous
speech supporting the ban on homosexuality in which he said: 'on
the ground of the Christian nature of our State and on the grounds
that the deliberate practice of homosexuality is morally wrong, that
it is damaging to the health both of individuals and the public and,
finally, that it is potentially harmful to the institution of marriage'.[1]

While the majority of the judges agreed with the Chief Justice, a
strong dissenting judgment was given by Judge McCarthy J, based
on the right to privacy. In his opinion, the ban was unconstitutional
because 'a very great burden lies upon those who would question
personal rights in order to justify State interference of a most grievous
kind (the policeman in the bedroom) in a claim to the right to
perform sexual acts or to give expression to sexual desires or needs in
private between consenting adults, male or female'.[2]

Norris appealed to the European Court of Human Rights, which
upheld his appeal in 1988, finding that the criminalisation of sexual
activity between men amounted to a breach of Article 8 of the
European Convention on Human Rights (the privacy guarantee),
because 'although members of the public who regard homosexuality

as immoral may be shocked, offended or disturbed by the commission by others of private homosexual acts, this cannot on its own warrant the application of penal sanctions when it is consenting adults alone who are involved'.[3] The European Court decision ultimately led to the repeal of the relevant legislation and the decriminalisation of homosexuality in the Criminal Law (Sexual Offences) Act 1993 – a mere twenty-five years ago. The *Norris* case represents an early example of the effective use by social campaigners in Ireland of international and European law mechanisms to achieve change. Reflecting on the case more recently in an edited collection of essays exploring how legal cases have been used to effect social change in Ireland, David Norris said that before initiating his legal action he had consulted with US campaigners, who had suggested to him that 'it's all about *how* you win, as much as what you win'. Thus, Norris initiated his action with a view to raising national consciousness through litigation strategy – in his own words, 'we wanted the case to attract as much razzmatazz as possible!'[4]

Decades of progressive social change for LGBT persons were to follow after the *Norris* case, with particular highlights being the inclusion in legislation of sexuality as a prohibited ground of discrimination in employment in 1998 and in the provision of goods and services in 2000; and the passage of civil partnership legislation in 2010.[5] These changes are detailed in this book, but Sonja Tiernan notes that the ultimate goal of marriage equality was only realised after further litigation was initiated, using the same strategies as the earlier *Norris* case.

That litigation was commenced in 2004, in the courageous case taken by Katherine Zappone and Ann Louise Gilligan seeking recognition in Ireland of their Canadian marriage and, as a consequence, the right to marry for gay couples in Ireland. They initiated a legal action following the refusal by the Irish tax authorities to recognise their marriage in Canada.[6] They built a successful advocacy campaign around the case, and raised a range of comparative and international law arguments during the hearings. They lost the case in the High Court before Judge Dunne, who ruled in December 2006 that

if there is in fact any form of discriminatory distinction between same sex couples and opposite sex couples by reason of the exclusion of same sex couples from the right to marry, then ... [one ground] of

justification must surely lie in the issue as to the welfare of children …
Until such time as state of knowledge as to the welfare of children is
advanced, it seems to me that the State is entitled to adopt a cautious
approach in changing the capacity to marry albeit that there is no
evidence of any adverse impact on welfare.[7]

This was a deeply disappointing judgment. Of course, the context
then was very different. At that point, civil partnership had not yet
been legalised in Ireland. Only a small number of US states had by
that time recognised marriage equality. But although the tide of
equality had not yet turned internationally, the High Court decision
still lacked logic. It ignored the nature of the right to marry and the
changing nature of the institution of marriage. An argument that
marriage must be confined to heterosexual couples because it was
'ever so' amounts to circular and illogical reasoning. The truth is that
the definition or meaning of marriage is not fixed in any society.
It has changed and evolved over time. And Sonja Tiernan does an
excellent job in these pages of documenting the changes in public
opinion brought about over time by the work of campaigners through
litigation, but also through political action.

Indeed, although we appealed the High Court decision in the
KAL litigation to the Supreme Court at the time, political developments soon overtook the legal action. Senator David Norris had
already been tabling legislation in the Seanad seeking recognition of
civil partnership; the day the High Court judgment in the KAL case
was given, as Sonja Tiernan notes, the Labour Party introduced a
further Civil Union Bill in the Dáil. Media appearances by Katherine
Zappone and Ann Louise Gilligan, and other gay couples, played a
large part in shifting public opinion; it gradually became clear that
the public wanted to see legal recognition of same-sex relationships.
The Civil Partnership Act, passed in 2010, provided that recognition;
but it fell short of equal provision, and was heavily criticised by many
campaigners, for whom full equality remained the goal.

And this goal was to be finally realised following the general
election of 2011 when, as Sonja Tiernan explains, Labour entered
government as a minority coalition partner with Fine Gael. The
Labour party, with an active Labour LBGT section, had championed
marriage equality in opposition, and in its 2011 election manifesto
committed to holding a referendum on this. At the time, Labour

leader Eamon Gilmore famously declared marriage equality to be 'the civil rights issue of this generation'.[8] The Fine Gael party accordingly agreed to the establishment of a Constitutional Convention to debate the merits of holding a referendum on same-sex marriage. That convention, made up of citizens and political representatives, of which I was proud to be a member, recommended by a large majority the holding of such a referendum. By this time, as Sonja Tiernan writes, the marriage equality campaign, set up to support the advocacy initiatives around the KAL case, was well established. Spokespersons and key leaders were already in place, strategies had been devised and the campaign was underway.

The referendum campaign itself was notable for the mobilisation of civil society and of large numbers of individuals who had never previously been politically active, but who turned out to canvass for the 'Yes Equality' alliance that led the campaign. This alliance promoted a positive message, based on telling the human stories behind the call for equality; prominent spokespersons spoke movingly of the impact of the ban on marriage upon their lives and the lives of their children. Political and public figures who had not previously spoken about their sexuality came out during the campaign for the first time; these included broadcaster Ursula Halligan and then government Minister, now Taoiseach, Leo Varadkar TD.

The passage of the referendum itself, marking the first popular vote for change on marriage equality internationally, marked a significant milestone in the journey to achieve what has indeed been a radical transformation in the lives of LGBT people in Ireland since the 1980s. But progressive change has not stopped there. Even since 2015, there have been further positive legislative developments on LGBT rights. In that year, the Equality (Miscellaneous Provisions) Act was passed, introducing changes which give gay teachers and other employees in religious-run schools and hospitals protection against discrimination and dismissal. Until that legislation was passed, discrimination was legally permitted if the lifestyle of teachers or other employees of such institutions was perceived to be in conflict with their employers' religious ethos. The Gender Recognition Act, passed the same year, provides legal recognition for transgender persons in Ireland for the first time. These two significant steps were both taken just months following the success of the referendum, again as Labour initiatives within government. And indeed, even since the election of a new government in 2016, other LGBT rights initiatives have been launched. An interdepartmental review of the Gender Recognition Act, to ensure that it adequately meets the needs of transgender persons, particularly young people, is already underway. My own legislation to provide equality for gay couples who have lost out on survivors' pension entitlements because they were legally unable to marry until after 2015 has been accepted by government; other Labour legislation providing for the quashing of convictions recorded prior to 1993 in respect of consensual adult sexual relations is also making progress.

But while we continue to work on these and other progressive legal changes, it is useful to reflect on the lessons from the marriage equality campaign, in understanding that while lawmaking and litigation can be a key strategy in achieving social change, there must also be public buy-in to make that change sustainable and truly embedded in social culture. As the 2015 campaign showed us, how we win is just as important as what we win. This book provides reflective consideration on the historical context for the campaign, as well as analysing how it was organised and what specific factors contributed to its winning outcome. Sonja Tiernan has done Irish society a great service in documenting *how* that win was brought about – a truly valuable lesson for generations to come.

## Notes

1 *Norris v the Attorney General* [1984] IR 36 (SC), at 65.
2 Ibid., at 102.
3 *Norris v. Ireland* [1988] ECHR 22, at para. 46.
4 Ivana Bacik and Mary Rogan (eds), *Legal Cases that Changed Ireland*, Dublin, 2016, p. 54.
5 The Employment Equality Act 1998; Equal Status Act 2000; Civil Partnership and Certain Rights and Obligations of Cohabitants Act 2010.
6 *Zappone & Gilligan v. Revenue Commissioners* [2006] IEHC 404, [2008] 2 IR 417 (HC). This author acted as junior counsel in the case.
7 Ibid., at 507.
8 Éamon Gilmore, *Inside the Room: The untold story of Ireland's crisis government*, Dublin, 2016, p. 216.

# Introduction:
# A social revolution begins

On Saturday 23 May 2015, events in Ireland shot onto the global stage. Televisions across the world beamed images of people taking to the streets of the capital city and across the twenty-six counties in celebration, in tears and in solidarity. Former President of Ireland, Mary McAleese, described it as a 'spontaneous carnival that broke out in Dublin Castle and the surrounding streets'.[1] Ireland had become the first country in the world to extend civil marriage to same-sex couples through a public vote. This was a momentous occasion for Ireland, and as Secretary General of the United Nations, Ban Ki-moon, declared, 'the result sends an important message to the world: all people are entitled to enjoy their human rights no matter who they are or whom they love'.[2]

This book records the political campaign and strategy that led to this momentous event, from the origins of a gay rights movement in a repressive Ireland through to the establishment of the Yes Equality campaign. The story traces how, for perhaps the first time in the history of the Irish State, the country shed its conservative Catholic image. Ultimately, this is the account of how a new wave of activism was successfully introduced in Ireland which has led to a social revolution that is now being fully realised through subsequent campaigns, activism and further referenda. The movement is best explored through the stories of the main campaigners, including those already well known in the Irish movement such as David Norris, Katherine Zappone and Ann Louise Gilligan, as well as individuals who inspired the founding of vibrant new groups such as Noise[3] and Marriage Equality or reactivated established groups such as the Gay and Lesbian Equality Network (GLEN). This social revolution is detailed through the accounts of how political lobbying was used and court cases were launched that brought about necessary legal and political change which now showcases Ireland as a progressive country continually working towards achieving full equality.

The referendum on marriage equality in 2015 is a central part of this struggle to achieve equality. Irish people turned up at the polls on Friday 22 May in record numbers to vote on whether or not to add one short sentence to the Irish Constitution: 'marriage may be contracted in accordance with law by two persons without distinction as to their sex'. The commitment of the people of Ireland to bring about this change for equality was evident in the overwhelming majority of Yes votes. Young and old; men and women; gay and straight; rural and urban; people across all religions and political parties voted overwhelmingly – Yes. Extending marriage to same-sex couples was viewed as a basic human right by Irish citizens. Those Irish citizens living abroad travelled from the four corners of the world to ensure they registered their Yes vote. The excitement on 23 May was the culmination of emotions that had in fact been building since earlier in the week when bands of Irish people arrived through ports and airports brandishing flags and badges emblazoned with 'Vote Yes'.

On Saturday morning, when the first polling boxes were opened for the count, various media sources began reporting excitedly how some boxes contained only Yes votes. This campaign and this result marked the beginning of a new wave of social reform in Ireland leading to other major events including the successful Repeal of the Eighth Amendment in 2018. Together for Yes orchestrated the repeal, and this group included many of the same campaigners in the Yes Equality movement including the leading feminist activist Ailbhe Smyth who in April 2019 was named on the Time 100 list.[4] This of course points to the significance of the marriage equality movement in Ireland. The movement and the campaigners continue to have a significant impact on subsequent social reform in the country.

However, the fact that Ireland required a referendum to allow abortion services as late as 2018 is telling. It was the people of Ireland who outlawed abortion in the country by voting to include an Eighth Amendment to the Irish Constitution in 1983. From that decision the life of the foetus became equal in Irish law to that of the mother through the words, 'the State acknowledges the right to life of the unborn and, with due regard to the equal right to the mother'.[5] Sixty-seven per cent of the Irish population voted to include this wording in law, ensuring women could not access abortion, under any circumstances, in Ireland. If a woman was forced to seek a termination, she must instead travel to Britain to access services there. This marked the all too familiar route of 1980s Catholic Ireland which offered an Irish solution to an Irish problem – export it to England. Indeed, while male homosexual activity remained a criminal offence in Ireland until 1993, many Irish gay men and also lesbians moved to England believing it was the only way they could live openly gay lives.

Such repressive ideas undoubtedly stemmed from the Catholic Church, which maintained a strong hold over the population of Ireland since the formation of the Irish Free State in 1922, and for decades afterwards interfered in the political governing of the country. The very cornerstone of the State was drafted in collusion with the Catholic hierarchy. The Irish Constitution, implemented in 1937, sets out the basic laws of the land, and it was written under the great influence of John Charles McQuaid, who later became Catholic Primate of Ireland and Archbishop of Dublin. Archbishop McQuaid continued to influence consecutive governments until his death in 1973. Even after McQuaid died, Catholic priests all too frequently directed their congregation from the pulpit on how to vote at upcoming referenda, especially when the issue concerned personal rights or family values.

The referendum on the issue of marriage equality in Ireland caused the Catholic Church much consternation. When the results were announced the Vatican Secretary of State, Cardinal Pietro Parolin, described it as a 'defeat for humanity'.[6] The Catholic Archbishop of Dublin, Diarmuid Martin, acknowledged that the Church 'have to stop and have a reality check, not move into denial of the realities'.[7] In the run-up to the 2015 referendum it was less likely for Catholic priests to direct their congregation on how to vote, and in instances where this happened people often walked out of the church in protest. However, there were numerous Catholic organisations and institutions such as the Iona Institute which actively, or some may say fiercely, campaigned against extending marriage to same-sex couples. Because the outcome of the referendum was so positive there has been a tendency to gloss over some negative elements of the campaign in the run-up to the 2015 referendum.

This book reveals how the referendum was hard fought and deeply disturbing for many individuals. It is important that this also becomes part of the following story. *Irish Times* journalist, Kathy Sheridan reported how an acquaintance of hers 'was called a c\*\*t on three occasions' while out canvassing for the Yes side. Such canvassers came from all walks of life, including a large number of heterosexual people who experienced bigotry and witnessed homophobia for the first time in their lives.[8] This book explores these issues in great detail using personal stories, legal cases, newspaper reports, social media engagement and parliamentary debates. This is the story of how a social revolution in Ireland began.

## Notes

1 Gráinne Healy, Brian Sheehan and Noel Whelan, *Ireland says Yes: The inside story of how the vote for marriage equality was won*, Dublin, 2016, p. xii.
2 Ed Carty and Noel Baker, 'Ban Ki-moon praises Ireland on marriage equality vote', *Irish Examiner* (24 May 2015).
3 An independent non-party group formed in 2007 to campaign for full equality for all people in Ireland regardless of gender or sexuality.
4 Ellen Coyne, 'Repeal leaders named icons for "transforming view of Ireland"', *The Times* (18 April 2019).
5 *Bunreacht na hÉireann* (Constitution of Ireland, enacted in 1937), Article 40.3.3 (ratified in 1983).
6 Paddy Agnew, 'Marriage referendum a "defeat for humanity" – does the Vatican just not get it?', *Irish Times* (30 May 2015).
7 Helen Nianias, 'Archbishop of Dublin Diarmuid Martin says yes vote for gay marriage shows weakening Catholic church in Ireland', *Independent* (24 May 2015).
8 Kathy Sheridan, 'Some Yes campaigners faced subtle, shocking bigotry', *Irish Times* (27 May 2015).

# 1

# Irish historical and global context

On 24 July 1975, David Norris, Chairman of the first national gay rights organisation, appeared on RTÉ's *Last House* television programme in an interview with co-host Áine O'Connor. Ireland was then the last remaining member of the European Economic Community to retain criminal penalties against male homosexual activity. In Ireland, homosexual men could still face legal penalties of imprisonment of between ten years to life for engaging in consensual sexual activity. These penalties stemmed from two archaic laws introduced while Ireland was under British rule: the Offences Against the Person Act 1861 and the Criminal Law Amendment Act 1885. The *Last House* discussion is thought to be the first interview with an openly gay man televised by the Irish national broadcaster RTÉ. The interview seemed to be an attempt to dispel what could now be termed as ignorant stereotyping of gay people.

Norris, then a lecturer at Trinity College Dublin, was Chair of the Irish Gay Rights Movement (IGRM) established the previous year with headquarters in Parnell Square in north Dublin inner city. Norris later described how, among many other roles, the group supported men arrested for homosexual offences and 'within a few years the numbers of arrests ... had dropped to virtually nil'.[1] The IGRM launched a number of protests and what gay rights campaigner, Kieran Rose described as 'occasional gay pickets outside the Department of Justice'.[2] Although arrests of gay men had virtually stopped during the 1970s, change was slow for advancing gay rights in Ireland more generally. Gay and feminist publications including *Gay News* and *Spare Rib* remained banned. In 1975 Dr Noel Browne, a previous Minister of Health and leader of the Progressive

Democrat party, then a serving Senator for the University of Dublin constituency, set about establishing that homosexuality was 'perfectly normal, but in our society it is a very crippling disability'.[3] Browne entered this assertion into a Seanad Éireann debate, the upper House of Parliament (Oireachtas), and he was condemned for it.

The IGRM split not long after it was founded. Norris led a new group, the Campaign for Homosexual Law Reform. The Campaign group comprised mainly law students, and they secured their first legal advisor among Norris's colleagues at Trinity College. Mary McAleese, then Reid Professor of Law and later President of Ireland, served as their legal advisor from 1975–79. McAleese's successor, Mary Robinson, was also appointed as Reid Professor of Penal Legislation, constitutional and criminal law, and the law of evidence, and became the first female President of Ireland. Norris sought and received the support of established politicians and social reformers as patrons. Noel Browne, the Very Reverend Victor Griffin Dean of St Patrick's Cathedral Dublin and the playwright Hugh Leonard all agreed to lend their names in support. In November 1977, the group led by Norris launched a legal challenge against the 1861 and 1885 laws, arguing that as these laws were enacted before the formation of the State and before the 1937 Irish Constitution was enacted, they should no longer be enforced.

The mention of the Constitution here is significant, as this would become the central issue in the campaign for the extension of marriage to same-sex couples. Ireland, like many States formed after a period of revolution, has a single written Constitution. When the Irish Free State was formed in 1922 a Constitution was adopted and underwent numerous and extensive amendments until 1936. Therefore a referendum was put to the people of Ireland to accept a new, more modern Constitution in 1937. The Irish Constitution (Bunreacht na hÉireann, which translates as the Basic Law of Ireland) was enacted by the people of Ireland on 1 July 1937. There were groups in opposition to its introduction, most notably the National University Women Graduates' Association which objected on the grounds that women were positioned as citizens with a specific social role, primarily defined by their family duties.[4] Nevertheless, the Constitution was carried by a popular vote. The document has been in operation since 29 December of that year and sets out, in two main sections, how Ireland should be governed and establishes the fundamental rights of

Irish citizens. The Irish Constitution includes fifty articles, of which 1–39 set out regulations ranging from the organisation of the government and the role of the Attorney General, to the control of the courts system. Articles 40–44 focus on fundamental rights including personal rights, the family, education, personal property and religion.

The Irish Constitution supersedes all other laws in the land. In theory all laws from before its introduction in 1937 should have been replaced, which was the basis of Norris's argument. The High Court ruled against Norris in *Norris v. The Attorney General*. On 10 October 1980, Justice McWilliam concluded that 'one of the effects of criminal sanctions against homosexual acts is to reinforce the misapprehension and general prejudice of the public and increase the anxiety and guilt feelings of homosexuals leading, on occasions, to depression and the serious consequences which can follow from that unfortunate disease'.[5] Regardless of the negative consequences of criminalising male homosexual activity, the case was dismissed on legal grounds that the criminalisation of male homosexual activity was not unconstitutional.

Norris appealed the decision to the Supreme Court. On 22 April 1983, the Supreme Court upheld the decision of the High Court by a majority of 3–2, concluding that:

> Public order and morality; the protection of the young, of the weak-willed, of those who may readily be subject to undue influence, and of others who should be deemed to be in need of protection; the maintenance inviolate of the family as the natural primary and fundamental unit of society; the upholding of the institution of marriage; the requirements of public health; these and other aspects of the common good require that homosexual acts be made criminal in many circumstances.[6]

During the Supreme Court challenge, the case of *Dudgeon v. United Kingdom* was referred to on numerous instances. Jeffrey Dudgeon's legal case related to Britain's decriminalisation of male homosexual activity, which was enacted through the introduction of the Sexual Offences Act in 1967. This legal change followed the recommendations of the Wolfenden Committee established a number of years earlier in August 1954. British authorities had become aware that the number of men imprisoned for homosexual activity had risen to an all-time high the previous year, with over one thousand arrests, and an inquiry was established. The Chair of the committee, John Wolfenden, published the 'Report on the Committee on Homosexual Offences and Prostitution' on 5 September 1957. Essentially Wolfenden recommended that it was not the business of the legal system or the State to interfere with the actions of consenting adults and homosexual activity should not therefore be a criminal offence. After much debate in the House of Commons over the following years the main recommendations of the report were enacted and homosexual activity in private was decriminalised in England and Wales for men above the age of twenty-one years. The age of consent set for homosexual male activity was considerably higher than the age of consent for heterosexual sex in Britain at the time, which was then sixteen years of age.

These legal updates were not extended to Northern Ireland, which still maintained the 1861 and 1885 laws, as in the Republic, making homosexual activity criminal offences punishable by imprisonment. Campaigners in the North founded the Northern Ireland Gay Rights Association (NIGRA) to contest this. In 1976, a number of those involved in the campaign, including the leader of NIGRA, Jeffrey Dudgeon, were arrested and questioned about their homosexual activities. Dudgeon, a citizen of Northern Ireland, stepped up the campaign for homosexual law reform which culminated in his legal action to the European Court of Human Rights, *Dudgeon v. United Kingdom*. The case was heard in Strasbourg claiming that criminalisation of homosexuality 'constituted an interference with a person's right to respect for his private life in contravention of Article 8 of the European Convention on Human Rights'.[7] The case concluded on 22 October 1981 with 15 votes to 4 agreeing that this was indeed a breach of the Convention on Human Rights. The findings forced a debate in the House of Commons and in October 1982 a law was passed decriminalising male homosexual activity in Northern Ireland. This law reform was most unwelcome to unionist politicians in the North of Ireland. Ian Paisley, leader and founder of the Democratic Unionist Party (DUP), had established the purposefully shockingly titled campaign, Save Ulster from Sodomy, in 1977 in direct opposition to the homosexual law reform campaign. In 2019, the DUP maintains its stance against equality for LGBT people and is the main opposition to extending marriage to same-sex couples in Northern Ireland.

The success of the decriminalisation case relating to Northern Ireland was used by Mary Robinson as senior counsel for David Norris. Robinson argued that the Supreme Court should regard the decision of the European Court of Human Rights 'as something more than a persuasive precedent and should be followed'.[8] The Supreme Court rejected this argument and found no reason to update the laws decriminalising homosexuality in Ireland. Norris and his legal team decided to move forward with their own challenge to the European Court of Human Rights.

In the meantime, the gay rights movement in Ireland was strengthening across the country. New organisations supporting and campaigning on behalf of lesbians and gay men were emerging at increasing rates. The main organisations included the Cork Irish Gay Rights Movement (1976); Liberation for Irish Lesbians (1978); The National Gay Federation (1979); Cork Gay Collective (1980); Dublin Gay Collective (1980); Galway Irish Gay Rights Movement and the Galway Gay Collective (1980); and the Cork Lesbian Collective (1983). Gay and lesbian centres shortly followed. On MacCurtain Street in Cork city, the Phoenix Club. In Dublin, the National Gay Federation opened a centre which they named after the German sexologist, Magnus Hirschfeld. The Hirschfeld Centre was located on Fownes Street, then a forgotten part of Dublin city, now part of the flamboyant Temple Bar area popular with tourists. It hosted much needed social spaces for lesbians and gay men to interact, including a café, a cinema and a disco called Flikkers. Such spaces also housed services such as counselling and community projects during the disturbing time which saw the onset of the AIDS crisis. These centres also became an important space for groups mobilising politically.

During the 1980s the gay rights movement became markedly more vibrant. In 1980, Joni Crone appeared on *The Late Late Show*, perhaps the most viewed television programme in Ireland at that time. Crone discussed her lesbian sexuality in an open and direct way on the Saturday night chat show with host Gay Byrne. The following year Liz Noonan stood for election as a Lesbian Feminist candidate. She was unsuccessful but stood again twice in 1982 in Dublin South East, increasing the visibility of lesbians in Ireland. Gay and lesbian telephone lines emerged to provide help and support for LGBT people around the country. Gay-friendly businesses opened such as Bookworm in Derry and the Quay co-op in Cork.

Against this background of energetic gay rights campaigning and community development David Norris issued his case to the European Court of Human Rights on 5 October 1983. While the case was ongoing Norris was elected to Seanad Éireann in 1987, becoming an independent Senator for the University of Dublin constituency. This election of the first openly gay Senator was testament to growing support for LGBT equal rights. Taking a similar approach to the Dudgeon case, Norris's team complained that the laws against homosexuality in Ireland breached Article 8 and that Norris 'suffered, and continues to suffer, an unjustified interference with his right to respect for his private life'.[9] Although the court recognised that Norris had not been subjected to any police investigation as Dudgeon had, Norris still faced restrictions in respect of his private life as he was a male homosexual and related activity was a criminal offence. On 26 October 1988, Norris, then still a Senator, won his case.

The 1988 European Court decision was a turning point in gay rights movements in Ireland. That same year the GLEN was founded by Kieran Rose and Christopher Robson to achieve social policy and legislative change for LGBT people. The decision of the European Court of Human Rights eventually led to the decriminalisation of male homosexual activity in the Republic of Ireland in 1993 through the introduction of the Criminal Law (Sexual Offences) Act. The bill had been proposed by then Fianna Fáil TD[10] and Minister for Justice, Máire Geoghegan-Quinn, during the short term of a Fianna Fáil and Labour Party coalition government under Albert Reynolds. The bill was finally enacted in June 1993.[11] As Yvonne Murphy points out, it was apt that 'Mary Robinson had been elected President of Ireland and it fell to her to sign the Bill into law'.[12]

The successes of political lobbying and organised campaigning ensured that Ireland then had a number of active advocate groups working towards equal rights for LGBT people. Decriminalisation of male homosexuality was only one element of the gay rights campaign. There was a recognition from within the LGBT community that gay men and lesbians needed to work together more closely. The National Gay Federation board voted in 1990 to change the group's name to the National Lesbian and Gay Federation (NLGF), a move that was supported by the vast majority of its members. The organisation had grown from strength to strength over the years and is still a vibrant and active group, renamed National LGBT Federation since 2014.

It founded the *Gay Community News*, a free paper carrying news for the gay community since February 1988 and still a hugely significant magazine for the LGBT community in Ireland.

Yvonne Murphy highlights the *Norris* case as a key time for LGBT equality legislation in Ireland. She describes how:

> A suite of other law reforms also followed the Norris judgement providing much-needed protections for members of the LGBT community under a range of headings, including the Incitement to Hatred Act, 1989, the Unfair Dismissals (Amendment) Act, 1993, the Refugee Act 1996 – which led the way internationally in including sexual orientation as a ground for granting refuge.[13]

In this vein, Ireland entered the twenty-first century with an optimistic focus on achieving equality for all of its citizens. The establishment of the Equality Authority on 18 October 1999 was broadly welcomed by social justice campaigners. The independent body replaced the, by then outdated, Employment Equality Agency. The Authority was granted a much extended role from its predecessor, overseeing the implementation of equality legislation which would 'work towards the elimination of discrimination' and also help 'promote equality' in employment and 'the provision of goods and services, accommodation and education'.[14] The legal basis for promoting equality and prohibiting discrimination was further enshrined in the Equal Status Act introduced just months later. The substance of the act ensured that an individual could not be 'treated less favourably' based on nine grounds. It was now illegal to discriminate against people in the provision of goods and services based on their gender, marital status, family status, sexual orientation, religion, age, disability, race or as a member of the Traveller community.[15]

This act, coupled with the Employment Equality Acts introduced in 1998 and 2004 which made it illegal to discriminate against workers based on sexual orientation, were significant developments towards equality for LGBT people in Ireland. However, a stipulation included in the Employment Equality Act highlighted how Ireland still held on to a deep-seated religious philosophy when forming laws. Section 37 of the 1998 act provided a legislative condition allowing religious-run institutions to discriminate against current or prospective employees, in accordance with their religious ethos. This section ensured that 'a religious, educational or medical institution which is under the direction or control of a body established for religious purposes' could discriminate against employing or continuing the employment of any person thought to undermine the religious ethos of the organisation.[16] This section effectively meant that any religious-run organisation could discriminate against a homosexual candidate during a recruitment process and, if employed, a gay or lesbian person could legally have their employment terminated solely because of their sexuality. The vast majority of State-funded schools and hospitals in Ireland remained under Church control when this law was introduced and therefore this equality legislation fell short of protecting many gay and lesbian employees.[17]

Meanwhile the effectiveness of the Equal Status Act in relation to protecting same-sex couples would be tested in 2003. In that year the Department of Social and Family Affairs refused to issue a free travel pass to the co-habiting partner of a gay man. The couple were effectively denied the same rights as their heterosexual equivalents in relation to the Free Travel Scheme operated by the Irish State. The Equality Authority intervened on behalf of the couple, citing this instance as a breach of the Equality Status Act. The Department was forced to accept that it had indeed breached the Act and a travel pass was duly issued to the man's partner. Both men received compensation and the Irish State, it seemed, was forced to grant equal entitlements to same-sex couples on a par with that offered to those in opposite-sex relationships.[18] The case received much media attention both in Ireland and abroad, often with sensational headlines such as 'travel pass for gay pensioner's lover'.[19] However, this was a significant case which could set a precedent in relation to State recognition of same-sex couples. Unfortunately this did not come to pass. The case only served to alert the government, then a coalition formed by Fianna Fáil and the Progressive Democrats under Bertie Ahern, to the fact that such couples could now legally demand rights and benefits equal to those received by opposite-sex co-habiting couples. This new equality had financial implications for State resources.

Then Fianna Fáil Minister for Social and Family Affairs, Mary Coughlan, was quick to act. In April 2004, the introduction of a new Social Welfare Act came into effect. The act included an insertion under 'provision in relation to certain administration schemes' which closed the loophole ensuring that State entitlements would now only be granted to eligible claimants and their spouse.[20] The fact that same-sex couples had no opportunity to legally marry in Ireland ensured that they would not be assessed as a couple in relation to State entitlements such as the Free Travel Scheme and Fuel Allowances. The new social welfare legislation effectively overturned the Equality Status Act. Senator Norris would later point out the contradictions of this case in a private Member's Motion on Human Rights Issues in Seanad Éireann. Noting that the government did not support human rights agencies, Norris described how 'the Government intervened legislatively to copper fasten the discrimination by redefining the word "spouse" specifically to exclude gay couples from the rights to which the very Equality Tribunal established by the Government decided they were entitled'.[21] This case simply highlights Murphy's claim that 'the rather narrow definition of the family that existed in Irish law during this period brought issues concerning the legal acknowledgement and accommodation of a variety of family structures to the fore. This included same-sex partnered families and a range of others, including lone and non-marital families.'[22]

In that same year of 2004, the Civil Registration Act was reviewed for the purposes of what was termed 'modernisation', to reflect changing laws. This act legislates for the registration of births, deaths and marriages, again under the direction of the Minister for Social and Family Affairs. The modernisation process was necessary to rationalise processes such as the registration of adoptions. The section relating to marriage was updated to ensure that legal registrations could extend the system to include such changes as decrees of divorce and nullity of marriage.[23] Such legislative changes recognising and allowing for marriage breakdown were a forward move in Ireland which, not coincidentally, were introduced under Bertie Ahern, who was the first and remains the only Taoiseach to have been legally separated from his wife. In establishing the main principles of what constituted a marriage, a section of the Civil Registration Act laid out five categories which caused an 'impediment to a marriage'. The fifth and final category related to marriage between same-sex couples and crudely stated that a marriage could not be recognised if 'both parties are of the same sex'. This insertion seemed somewhat antiquated at a time when other jurisdictions were updating laws to make way for full access to civil marriage for same-sex couples. To add to this insult, the insertion led on from an old stipulation that a 'marriage would be void by virtue of the Marriage of Lunatics Act 1811'.[24] The insertion effectively established a ban on same-sex couples from marrying and yet such a major change in legislation was introduced without debate in either the Dáil Éireann, the lower House of the Oireachtas and principal chamber, or in the Seanad. Indeed, the updated legislation did not draw any real public attention until a High Court case two years later.

In the midst of these changes to Irish legislation which ensured same-sex couples were further denied legal recognition, a bigger case was brewing against the State. The case would propel the issue of marriage equality into the public arena and generate high-profile political and legal debate across Ireland. On 13 September 2003, two Irish citizens, Drs Katherine Zappone and Ann Louise Gilligan, were married in Vancouver, British Columbia, Canada in a legally binding civil ceremony. Zappone, then a lecturer in theology, ethics and education at Trinity College Dublin also served as a commissioner with the Irish Human Rights Commission (IHRC) (2002–12). She was born in the State of Washington, USA and became an Irish citizen in 1995. Gilligan, then a theologian teaching at Saint Patrick's College, part of Dublin City University, was a member of the Statutory Committee on Educational Disadvantage. Gilligan was born in Dublin and initially became a nun in the Loreto Convent. Gilligan and Zappone met and fell in love while studying for their doctorates in theology at Boston College in America. The couple were highly educated and were experienced community activists. In 1986, the women established The Shanty, run by a committee of women and later developed into An Cósan (The Path), an adult education project based in the working-class Dublin district of Jobstown, Tallaght.

Zappone and Gilligan married in Canada because marriage had been extended to same-sex couples in British Columbia earlier that year and was offered to people without any citizenship requirements. The introduction of this legislation in British Columbia was the result of an intense legal campaign by the marriage equality movement which was now spreading across Canada and America. Campaigns were launched in several states, legally challenging the constitutionality of denying same-sex couples the right to marry. The case for introducing marriage equality in Canada had been fought through a number of provincial court cases and by 2003 legislation had been passed in nine provinces across the Canadian territories.[25] The court cases were led, in the main, by LGBT and social justice organisations which challenged various aspects of the Constitution on equality grounds.

The ground-breaking case for Canada occurred in 1999 when the Supreme Court ruled that same-sex couples should have similar entitlements to married couples. The ruling was in response to a case taken by a lesbian couple in Ontario in 1998 which challenged the definition of 'spouse'. The couple appealed on the basis that the Family Law Act in Canada extends rights to unmarried opposite-sex couples and the 'failure to provide [the] same rights to members of same-sex couples infringes [on the] right to equality'.[26] The respondents were supported by numerous organisations named as interveners in the case.[27] The ruling in this case provided same-sex couples many more legal and financial entitlements but fell short of anything close to marriage.

The challenge to extend marriage to same-sex couples in Canada was brought forward in November 2001 when two cases were heard by the Ontario Superior Court of Justice. The first case was taken by eight same-sex couples who made applications to the Clerk of the City of Toronto for civil marriage licences. The Clerk did not issue the licences but informed the couples that she would apply to the court for legal clarification. The couples proceeded with an application to the court on 22 August 2000. Within months two same-sex couples were married in a joint ceremony, attended by over one thousand people at the Metropolitan Community Church in Toronto.[28] The Canadian government would not recognise the marriages and refused to issue licences. The Church applied to the court in the State of Ontario with a challenge to the decision.

The cases were supported by the intervention of EGALE Canada Inc., a national equality rights group. The decision was published in July 2002; the three judges unanimously concluded that the common law bar to same-sex marriage breached the equality rights of LGBT people under Section 15 of the Canadian Charter of Rights and Freedoms.[29] The court instructed Ontario to comply with its decision and extend civil marriage to same-sex couples within a two-year period. As was anticipated, the federal government appealed the decision of the court. A hearing took place in the Court of Appeal for Ontario between 22 and 25 April 2003, which involved seven couples and the Metropolitan Community Church of Toronto as respondents.[30] Again, a number of organisations intervened to support the case for marriage equality.[31] The central question in the case focused on the exclusion of same-sex couples from the common law definition of marriage. In Canada the definition of marriage was based on a case heard by Lord Penzance in the English Court of Probate and Divorce, as far back as 1866, in which it was stated that marriage 'may for this purpose be defined as the voluntary union for life of one man and one woman, to the exclusion of all others'.[32]

In the introduction to the appeal case a synopsis point describes marriage from a contemporary perspective which animates exquisitely why it is of such importance to grant all people equal access to marriage:

> Marriage is, without dispute, one of the most significant forms of personal relationships. For centuries, marriage has been a basic element of social organization in societies around the world. Through the institution of marriage, individuals can publicly express their love and commitment to each other. Through this institution, society publicly recognizes expressions of love and commitment between individuals, granting them respect and legitimacy as a couple. This public recognition and sanction of marital relationships reflect society's approbation of the personal hopes, desires and aspirations that underlie loving, committed conjugal relationships. This can only enhance an individual's sense of self-worth and dignity.[33]

Taking this perspective into consideration, the three judges presiding at the Court of Appeal upheld the decision of the Divisional Court. The judges determined unanimously that the existing definition of marriage was unconstitutional and that this contravened the equality rights set out in the Canadian Charter of Rights and Freedoms. The court ruled that the definition of marriage should be replaced with non-gender-specific language defining it as 'the voluntary union for life of two persons to the exclusion of all others'. Marriage between same-sex couples thus became legal in Ontario on 10 June 2003, closely followed by civil marriage equality in British Columbia on 8 July that year. In 2005, the Civil Marriage Act was introduced by the Federal Government of Canada, legalising same-sex marriage across the entirety of Canada.

Similar methods to achieve marriage equality were also applied in America. GLAD (GLBTQ Legal Advocates and Defenders) applied to the court contesting the constitutionality of not extending civil marriage to same-sex couples. On 11 April 2001, GLAD initiated a case on behalf of seven couples in Massachusetts.[34] This case reached the Supreme Court, where the judges also ruled that it was unconstitutional not to extend civil marriage to same-sex couples. On 17 May 2004, Massachusetts became the first American state to legislate for marriage equality. Cases to legalise marriage to same-sex couples were brought against states all across America. By 2015, all but fourteen American states had introduced marriage equality. In June of that year the US Supreme Court ruled that marriage is a legal right to all couples across the entire USA, legalising marriage equality across all fifty states.

Although marriage equality cases across Canada and the United States gained more international media exposure, the campaign first began within the European Union. The first country to introduce marriage for same-sex couples was the Netherlands in 2001. Belgium followed suit in 2003, ensuring that not only Belgian nationals but also foreigners living in Belgium could marry. This was followed by a series of countries across the globe extending full marriage rights to same-sex couples. In 2005, Spain shed its image as a Catholic-dominated country by introducing full marriage rights to same-sex couples and in 2006 South Africa became the first African country to extend this same equality. Norway and Sweden both changed their laws to accommodate full marriage to all in 2009.

Portugal, Iceland and Argentina extended marriage to same-sex couples in 2010, with the Prime Minister of Iceland, Johanna Sigurdardottir, taking advantage of this long-awaited legislation by marrying her long-term female partner that year. Denmark followed suit in 2012 and the following year Brazil, France, Uruguay and New Zealand all introduced legislation granting marriage to same-sex couples. The Marriage (Same Sex Act) 2014 was introduced in England and Wales, with the first marriages taking place that year, and quickly followed by Scotland; leaving Northern Ireland as the only jurisdiction in the UK not to allow marriage between same-sex couples. Luxembourg introduced full marriage equality in 2015. The trend continued and in April 2016 Columbia's highest court ruled that marriage should not be restricted to opposite-sex couples; within the same week Greenland also legalised marriage to same-sex couples. Finland approved a bill legalising marriage equality which was signed by its President and came into effect on 1 March 2017.

The table on marriage equality across the globe in the preliminary material details the global situation as of April 2019.

## Notes

1 As cited in Brian Lacey, *Terrible Queer Creatures*, Dublin, 2008, p. 246.
2 Ibid.
3 Brendan Kelly, *Hearing Voices: The history of psychiatry in Ireland*, Dublin, 2016, p. 315.
4 For more on gender concerns in the Irish Constitution see Sonja Tiernan, 'Countess Markievicz and Eva Gore-Booth', in Eugenio Biagini and Daniel Mulhall (eds), *The Shaping of Modern Ireland: A centenary assessment*, Dublin, 2016, pp. 185–97.
5 *Norris v. A.G.* [1983] IESC 3; [1984] IR 36 (22 April 1983).
6 Ibid.
7 *Dudgeon v. United Kingdom*, Series A, No. 45, Before the European Court of Human Rights (23 September 1981).
8 *Norris v. A.G.*
9 *Norris v. Ireland*, Application no. 10581/83, European Court of Human Rights, Strasbourg (26 October 1988).
10 Teachta Dála, an elected member of Dáil Éireann; the British equivalent is a Member of Parliament.
11 The bill passed the Dáil on 24 June and the Seanad on 30 June 1993. See Craig Dwyer (ed.), *Gay Law Reform Debates 1993: Dáil and Seanad*, Dublin, 2013.
12 Yvonne Murphy, 'The marriage equality referendum 2015', *Irish Political Studies*, 31:2 (2016), 317.
13 Ibid.
14 Judy Walsh, Catherine Conlon, Barry Fitzpatrick and Ulf Hansson, *Enabling Lesbian, Gay and Bisexual Individuals to Access Their Rights under Equality Law: A report prepared for the Equality Commission for Northern Ireland and the Equality Authority* (November 2007).
15 Equal Status Act (2000) Section 3 (2).
16 Employment Equality Act (1998) Section 37 (1).
17 After much campaigning by LGBT groups this section was finally overturned in December 2015. The Equality (Miscellaneous Provisions) Bill 2013 amending the provisions of Section 37 (1) of the Employment Equality Act was passed by the Dáil on 2 December 2015.
18 Equality Authority, *Annual Report 2003*, Dublin, 2004.
19 Rod Chayter, *The Mirror* (26 September 2003).
20 Social Welfare Act (2004) Section 19, 245B (1).

21  David Norris, *Private Member's Motion*, Seanad Éireann (6 February 2009).
22  Murphy, 'Marriage equality referendum 2015', 317.
23  Civil Registration Act No. 3 (2004).
24  Ibid., Part 1, Section 2 (e).
25  In 2005, the Canadian government introduced a bill legalising marriage equality nationwide, across all thirteen provinces.
26  *M. v. H.* [1999] 2 SCR 3, 1999 CanLII 686 (SCC).
27  The Foundation for Equal Families, the Women's Legal Education and Action Fund, Equality for Gays and Lesbians Everywhere (EGALE), the Ontario Human Rights Commission, the United Church of Canada, the Evangelical Fellowship of Canada, the Ontario Council of Sikhs, the Islamic Society of North America, Focus on the Family and REAL Women of Canada.
28  Two couples – Kevin Bourassa and Joe Varnell; and Elaine and Anne Vautour – were married in the Metropolitan Community Church in Toronto on 14 January 2001.
29  The presiding judges were Associate Chief Justice Heather F. Smith, Regional Senior Justice Robert A. Blair and Justice Harry LaForme.
30  The couples involved in the suit were: Hedy Halpern and Colleen Rogers; Michael Leshner and Michael Stark; Aloysius Pittman and Thomas Allworth; Dawn Onishenko and Julie Erbland; Carolyn Rowe and Carolyn Moffatt; Barbara McDowall and Gail Donnelly; and Alison Kemper and Joyce Barnett. One couple had split up after the initial case was brought to court.
31  The intervenors: EGALE Canada Inc.; Metropolitan Community Church of Toronto; the Interfaith Coalition on Marriage and Family; the Association for Marriage and the Family in Ontario; Canadian Coalition of Liberal Rabbis for Same-Sex Marriage; and the Canadian Human Rights Commission.
32  *Halpern et al v. Attorney General Canada*, [2003] O.J. No. 2268.
33  Ibid.
34  *Goodridge v. Dept. of Public Health*, 798 N.E.2d 941 (Mass. 2003).

# 2

# The path to the High Court

Katherine Zappone and Ann Louise Gilligan were tracking the development and successes of the marriage equality movement globally. The couple, together since 1981, held a life-partnership ceremony to celebrate their commitment to each other in October 1982. It would be over thirty years before they could legally marry, and then not in their country of residence. Zappone and Gilligan were married in British Columbia just over two months after the marriage equality legislation was implemented there. By that stage they had already determined that a legal challenge should be pursued in Ireland, ideally through similar methods used by activists in Canada and America.

In 2002, Zappone and Gilligan began a process which would ultimately bring the issue of marriage equality in Ireland to the fore. In April of that year, Zappone contacted the Equality Authority for advice on how to proceed with a case to establish legal recognition of her and Gilligan's partnership. While supportive of the couple, ultimately the Equality Authority found that this case was not within its remit. The Authority was tasked with prohibiting discrimination in employment and in the provision of goods and services.[1] The two women were keen to pursue their goal in solidarity with the wider community and sought out other support. They met with Ailbhe Smyth, a feminist activist, founder and then Director of the Women's Education, Resource and Research Centre at University College Dublin and then also Co-chair of the NLGF. Smyth advised Zappone and Gilligan to meet with Christopher Robson of GLEN. Robson, a steadfast campaigner for LGBT equality, was working with Senator Norris on establishing a draft for a Domestic Partnership Bill.[2] Both of these men were adept equality activists.

Moving forward after his success with decriminalising male homosexual activity in Ireland, Norris now planned to introduce a Domestic Partnership Bill into the Seanad. His planned bill did not focus specifically on same-sex partnerships but included provisions for all co-habiting couples. If introduced, the bill would extend further rights, mainly in relation to financial and tax issues, to co-habiting couples. Zappone later described how, to herself and Gilligan, 'the bill in question read more like a proposal for a business contract between two people who co-habit, something which did not at all reflect the nature of our life-partnership'.[3] This was to become a divide within LGBT community groups, some of whom were satisfied with partnership rights while others held fast to seeking full marriage.

After much consideration Zappone and Gilligan decided that the only way forward was to seek legal advice. In May 2003, the couple were first introduced to Ivana Bacik, then Reid Professor of Law at Trinity College Dublin and a barrister-at-law.[4] Within two months the couple resolved to take legal action to have their partnership recognised in Ireland. By then they had secured an impressive legal team, who in full support of this equality issue agreed to work on a pro bono, no fee, basis. The team comprised Bacik as junior counsel, her colleague Gerard Hogan as senior counsel and Phil O'Hehir acting as their solicitor. After Zappone and Gilligan's Canadian marriage in September 2003, their legal team stepped up activities. That same month the Equality Authority completed a research brief on their case. It concluded that although the Equal Status Act could not overturn laws already in place in Ireland, a constitutional case could be taken to challenge legislation that discriminated against same-sex couples. Legal advisor to the Equality Authority, Eilis Barry, observed that Zappone and Gilligan could challenge legislation which discriminated against them 'on the basis of Article 40.1 of the Constitution which guarantees persons "equality before the law" and also on the basis of Article 40.3 which protects the rights of privacy and dignity for all Irish citizens'.[5]

The couple's legal team considered the Equality Authority's report and it was agreed that Zappone and Gilligan would pursue a legal challenge. It was decided to follow the course of action successfully taken by so many internationally. The women sought other couples who, along with them, would apply for a marriage licence in Ireland. This approach of using multiple couples had proven successful, including in Canada where Zappone and Gilligan were married. The search for others willing to be part of this legal challenge is described by Zappone and Gilligan as 'one extremely disheartening dead end'.[6] There are many reasons, possibly based on personal issues, why others did not join this legal challenge but ultimately the lack of response highlights that achieving civil marriage equality was not yet perceived as a significant goal of LGBT organisations in Ireland at that time.

Months passed by without any solid progress. In February 2004, it was time to consider a different strategy. Senior counsel, Hogan, outlined a new tactic. The couple were already legally married in Canada and therefore they could apply to the Revenue Commissioners in Ireland for a change in tax status. On 26 April 2004, Zappone and Gilligan duly alerted the Revenue Commissioners of their change in circumstance. In the letter to the Commissioners they enclosed a certificate of their marriage and an affidavit of the validity of the same signed by Kenneth W. Smith, a Canadian barrister and solicitor. The women simply requested, as taxpayers, that they receive the same financial allowances and appraisal as that offered to opposite-sex married couples living in Ireland.

The Revenue Commissioners sent a courteous, yet perplexed response on 1 July. In the letter, addressed 'Dear Ladies', they noted that this was the first time that they had received such a request. They refused to recognise Zappone and Gilligan as a married couple for tax purposes, noting that 'Irish taxation legislation caters for marriage only on the basis of the institution consisting of a husband and wife'. They continued that although 'the Taxes Acts do not define husband and wife, the *Oxford English Dictionary* offers the following:

> *Husband* – a married man especially in relation to his wife
> *Wife* – a married woman especially in relation to her husband.'[7]

Zappone and Gilligan were not surprised at the response from the Revenue Commissioners. It was unlikely that the State body would alter its tax returns in recognition of their marriage. This now meant that the women could prepare a case to challenge the Revenue Commissioners' decision.

In this way the KAL Advocacy Initiative was born; the name of the group based on the initials of the first names of Katherine Zappone and Ann Louise Gilligan. The couple did not act on a whim when deciding to pursue a legal challenge. They had carefully considered the implications of bringing a high-profile challenge which would impact on their social, financial and professional lives. A challenge was brought by judicial review, a process through which the High Court was requested 'to review the decision made by the Revenue Commission not to allow their claim for tax allowances, based on the *Oxford English Dictionary's* definition of "husband" and "wife"'.[8] Permission to launch the challenge was granted by Mr Justice Liam McKechnie on 9 November 2004.

While the KAL legal team agreed to work on a no fee basis, taking a legal challenge to the High Court still had substantial financial implications, particularly if they lost the case. In the event that Zappone and Gilligan lost their plea, they could be ordered to pay the State's legal costs. The Atlantic Philanthropies provided financial support, awarding the initiative €80,000 in 2005. Atlantic was established by entrepreneur Chuck Feeney to help 'advance opportunity and lasting change for those who are unfairly disadvantaged'.[9] Therefore, the philanthropic organisation was keen to support the cause, noting it would help 'improve the access of co-habiting couples to their rights by providing support for the KAL Advocacy Initiative which seeks the establishment of civil partnership legislation in Ireland'.[10]

While Gilligan and Zappone were fighting to have their marriage recognised in Ireland, the case for civil partnerships was progressing, separately. Senator Norris had established an advisory committee on civil partnerships in 2004. In December of that year he tabled a Private Members Civil Partnership Bill in Seanad Éireann. The bill proposed a legal registration for civil partnerships between two adults either of the same sex or of the opposite sex.[11] The bill reached the second stage debate on 16 February 2005. Significantly, in the debate Independent Senator Joe O'Toole, for the National University of Ireland (NUI) constituency, highlighted that there could be no comparisons drawn between marriage and civil partnership. O'Toole supported Norris's Civil Partnership Bill and stated that this 'does not constitute gay marriage or any innovative or new kind of marriage. This bill is what it claims to be and we get what it says on the tin, namely, civil registration. It represents a necessary response to the extraordinarily varied relationships which exist and develop in modern society.'[12] However, the Minister of Justice, Equality and Law Reform, then member of the Progressive Democrats, Michael McDowell, pointed to the KAL case as playing a significant part regarding legislating for civil partnership. McDowell, a trained barrister, had recently served as Attorney General of Ireland from 1999 to 2002 and was well aware of the implications, stating that 'it is of interest whether the Supreme Court rules that two gay people who are married abroad can have their marriage recognised here, as is now being ventilated in the courts.'[13]

After the Seanad debate it was agreed that the bill would not be given a second reading so that three main issues could be further considered. In the first instance, it was deemed pertinent to await the results of the Gilligan and Zappone case to ascertain if the State would indeed recognise their foreign marriage. Secondly, it was agreed to consider the findings of the All-Party Oireachtas Committee on the Constitution which was currently examining articles relating to the family. The Senators expressed a concern that the introduction of a Civil Partnership Bill would directly challenge the meaning of family as defined by the Irish Constitution. A final consideration was the outcome of the Report of the Law Reform Commission on the Rights and Duties of Cohabitees. The report was the second phase of a programme of law reform, stemming from a consultation paper which had made recommendations for reform of the law relating to co-habitants, either opposite- or same-sex couples.

It seemed that the marriage equality debate being pushed by Gilligan and Zappone was now almost being replaced by a discussion on civil partnership. Indeed, later that year the first same-sex civil partnership on the island of Ireland would take place. On 19 December 2005, Shannon Sickles and Grainne Close became the first couple to publicly register their relationship under the UK civil partnership laws. The ceremony took place in Belfast City Hall. The fact that the first UK civil partnership ceremony took place on the island of Ireland seemed to make this issue all the more urgent in the Republic of Ireland.

That same month Minister McDowell announced that he would establish a Working Group on Domestic Partnerships. The group was established in March 2006 and was tasked with laying out options as to how the State should treat co-habiting couples. The focus was not limited to the situation regarding same-sex couples but also included opposite-sex couples and those in non-conjugal relationships. McDowell invited a previous affiliate of his political party to chair the group. Anne Colley, a former Progressive Democrat TD was also a trained solicitor and the outgoing Chairperson of the Legal Aid Board. The members of the working group included numerous civil servants from various government departments including Justice, Equality and Law Reform; Finance; Social and Family Affairs; Health and Children; and from the Office of the Attorney General. Eilis Barry of the Equality Authority, Eoin Collins of GLEN and Dervla Browne of the Family Lawyers Association were also included in the working group, as was the economist Finola Kennedy, a committed advocate of Catholicism.

While the Colley group was in the planning stages of its first public dialogue on domestic partnerships, GLEN launched an ambitious five-year plan, the *Building Sustainable Change Programme*.[14] GLEN described its goals as 'an action programme to deliver equality and inclusion for lesbian, gay and bisexual people' and clearly established that it intended to participate fully with the Colley group 'to examine models of legal recognition of same-sex partnership'.[15] The Fianna Fáil Taoiseach, Bertie Ahern, accepted an invitation to launch the programme at GLEN's offices in Dublin. This was a momentous occasion, marking the first official attendance of a Taoiseach at an LGBT event. Ahern's speech at the launch was a landmark statement about equality for LGBT people. In it he declared:

> Our sexual orientation is not an incidental attribute. It is an essential part of who and what we are. All citizens, regardless of sexual orientation, stand equal in the eyes of our laws. Sexual orientation cannot, and must not, be the basis of a second-class citizenship. Our laws have changed, and will continue to change, to reflect this principle.[16]

However, Bertie Ahern also pointed to the possible challenges of introducing civil partnerships in line with the British model. Although the speech was a short statement, it provides an insight to the early views of the Fianna Fáil and Progressive Democrat coalition government of the day. This was one of the earliest mentions by a head of government regarding constitutional issues and the legal recognition of same-sex relationships. Ahern identified the fact that Ireland has a single written Constitution as a cause of complication to introducing civil partnerships. Moreover, although he recognised civil marriage as an issue raised by GLEN in its five-year programme, the Taoiseach discussed how the government might work towards the introduction of civil partnerships and was careful not to mention extending civil marriage to same-sex couples. The expressions by the Taoiseach were echoed the next month by Minister McDowell, who was to become Tánaiste (Deputy Prime Minister) shortly afterwards.

McDowell made his views clear at the launch of the Legal Status of Cohabitants and Same-Sex Couples conference in May. The Colley group organised the conference along with GLEN and the Equality Authority. The organisers set out clear aims to establish debate on the status of co-habiting couples in Ireland with the intention of informing the Working Group on Domestic Partnerships which in turn could recommend steps to shape a new status for such couples.[17] An impressive list of speakers was secured, including Claire L'Heureux Dube, a former justice in the Supreme Court of Canada, who served during the period that marriage equality was achieved there; Beatriz Gimeno, a political activist and President of the Spanish Federation of Lesbians, Gays, Transexuals and Bisexuals, again a position held during the time that Spain introduced marriage equality; and Brenda Marjorie Hale, Rt Hon. The Baroness Hale Richmond DBE, who was the first woman to hold the position of Lord of Appeal in Ordinary in the House of Lords. Other speakers included notable academics such as Kees Waaldijk, later a Professor of Comparative Sexual Orientation Law at the Universiteit Leiden.

The conference was held at the Royal College of Physicians on Kildare Street in Dublin on 26 May 2006. McDowell took to the podium to launch the conference, declaring how 'a political consensus is emerging towards legislating in this area and I am committed to building on this consensus by bringing forward legislative proposals during the lifetime of this Government'.[18] The *Irish Examiner* reported how a 'mini riot' ensued during which six men threw water, cups and copies of the Constitution at McDowell before eventually leaving the premises.[19] Eoin Collins, then Director of Policy Change at GLEN, explained that this was led by members of the Ancient Order of Hibernians (AOH), who had taken up positions in the audience.[20] The AOH is an Irish Catholic organisation that was established in New York in 1836 and now has branches across the globe, including in Ireland. Only men are allowed as primary members of the organisation, although a division for ladies has been established; other requirements for membership include being a practising Catholic and of Irish heritage. The AOH has a history of displaying a homophobic ethos, most evident when it banned the Irish Lesbian and Gay Organisation from marching under its banner in the 1992 New York St Patrick's Day parade.

Once McDowell was allowed to continue speaking, in his opening address he clarified his intention to concentrate on civil partnership entitlements rather than on full marriage, noting how:

> many same-sex couples may not want an institution which gives them all the rights, entitlements and duties of marriage. Married people owe each other many judicially enforceable duties such as a duty on maintenance, a special duty in respect of any home used by them and many other duties. Married status also involves other legal issues such as judicial competence over capital assets, divorce, competence as a witness, subjection to family law and other legal consequences. Same-sex couples may prefer a form of civil partnership which protects certain rights of importance to them.[21]

Indeed in his interview with the *Irish Examiner*, McDowell not only confirmed his ideas of what he thought same-sex couples wanted, but also stressed his view that 'the vast majority of gay men' did not want marriage.[22] The logic behind this assumption was later dealt with by Eoin Collins in his address to the conference. Collins noted how 'it seems reasonable to suppose that there are some lesbian and gay people who may not want to marry, just as there are some heterosexual people who may not want to marry. But there are many lesbian and gay people who do wish to take on the rights and obligations of marriage and who want the option to do so.'[23]

One couple who were vocal about wanting legal recognition of their marriage was Zappone and Gilligan. Their case had a full hearing in the High Court commencing on 3 October 2006. A gathering was organised for that same day, crowds assembled outside Dáil Éireann to highlight the public support for legal recognition of all relationships, equally. The High Court challenge to the Revenue Commissioners was the basis used to initiate this court case but ultimately the case challenged the very basis of State legislation which denied civil marriage to same-sex couples and therefore did not value homosexual people as equal citizens in Ireland. Zappone describes the basis of the case:

> Our primary legal arguments included that homosexual identity is a normal way of being human and that as such we have a human right to marry the person we choose to love. We argued that this right is implicit within the Irish Constitution and that the Constitution, which does not define marriage as between a man and a woman, also guarantees us equality before the law. We were of the view that the Constitution could be re-interpreted to recognise our Canadian marriage, otherwise our human rights are not protected and we are being discriminated against because of our sexual identity.[24]

The trial was heard by Ms Justice Elizabeth Dunne. The KAL legal team comprised Michael Collins SC, Gerard Hogan SC and Ivana Bacik BL, who were instructed by Phil O'Hehir of Brophy Solicitors. The team laid out a clear argument that Zappone and Gilligan were entitled to have their marriage legally recognised in Ireland based on four main points. First, that there was no need to change the wording of the Irish Constitution to allow for inclusion of marriage between same-sex couples. The Irish Constitution, they argued, is a 'living document ... open to reinterpretation'. In other words, 'the current understanding of marriage should not be limited to "a union between a man and a woman" simply because that is how it has always been defined'.[25] Secondly, the KAL legal team highlighted that by denying the right to civil marriage in this instance, the State was also denying the children of same-sex couples the benefits of having their families legally recognised. Furthermore, by prohibiting two consenting adults from marrying, the State was creating discrimination based on sexual orientation. Finally, it was argued that although opposite-sex co-habiting couples were taxed as unmarried single people, heterosexual couples were given the choice to marry if they so wished.

The Revenue Commissioners and the Attorney General were represented by a legal team comprising Paul Gallagher SC, Donal O'Donnell SC and Douglas Clarke BL, under the instruction of Fiona Woodyatt for the Chief State Solicitor's Office. The defendants responded to each of the main arguments. In relation to the Irish Constitution, it was argued that the term 'marriage' was intended to refer to the legal relationship between a man and a woman and that this was unambiguous. On the issue of children of same-sex couples, the defendants argued that there was no thorough evidence that such a family structure was in the best interests of children. The legal team presented an opinion that marriage laws in Ireland were already established for opposite-sex couples and this did not represent discrimination against same-sex couples. Finally, relating to discrimination on tax grounds, the defendants argued that as Zappone and Gilligan were taxed the same as unmarried co-habiting couples, there was no discrimination. Numerous experts were called to support the arguments on both sides. The trial attracted immense media attention and national newspapers such as the *Irish Independent* featured articles related to the case on a daily basis. Headlines in that paper seemed to favour the case put forward by Zappone and Gilligan, announcing how 'married lesbians affirm their love while in court' and how the court was told that there was 'no difference if children raised by lesbian parents'.[26]

The High Court case taken by Zappone and Gilligan was an intense challenge to the structures through which same-sex couples were denied legal recognition of committed relationships. The case was still ongoing when the *Options Paper presented by the Working Group on Domestic Partnership* was published in November 2006. The findings are now commonly referred to as the 'Colley Report'. In her foreword to the report, Anne Colley acknowledged how the working group examined issues relating to co-habiting couples in general but, she stressed, 'to same-sex couples in particular'.[27] Colley further acknowledged that it was difficult to assess the exact numbers of people affected by the lack of legal recognition of their relationship. The working group was reliant on census returns to gauge the number of same-sex couples living in Ireland. On previous census forms a question was included asking each person living in a household to affirm their relationship to the head of that household and to identify their gender. In the 1996 census returns only 150 co-habiting same-sex couples were identifiable. This number increased in the following returns of 2002 which identified 1,300 same-sex couples living together. Even the increase in the 2002 returns seemed particularly low bearing in mind that there were approximately 77,000 co-habiting couples reported on the census that year. Colley herself suggested that this was due to a number of reasons, mainly fear by lesbians and gay men that if they disclosed their sexuality they would be subjected to discrimination or prejudice.[28]

The Colley Report was clear from the outset that, unlike the financial basis of civil partnership options, lack of legal recognition of a same-sex partnership was all-encompassing and denied homosexual couples equality on many levels. In the section dedicated to same-sex couples it was stated in the introduction that 'lack of legal recognition also has very practical and direct consequences for LGB families because they are excluded from the benefits and legally enforceable obligations that are available through civil marriage'.[29] The group considered co-parenting issues for same-sex couples and addressed concerns in relation to a range of demographics ranging from young lesbians and gay men to the elderly.

The report set out the 'Direct Implications of Existing Legal Status' for same-sex couples. This was the first time that a government report had detailed the consequences of denying civil marriage to gay and lesbian partnerships. The report noted that same-sex couples were discriminated against in a range of basic areas, including in the provision of pensions and workplace benefits, allowing for joint adoption, in access to housing and succession of tenancy, succession rights, for property rights upon breakdown of a relationship, when establishing co-habitation contracts regulating property entitlements and in the allocation of tax allowances, both income and for capital taxes.[30]

The Colley Report highlighted how denying legal recognition for same-sex couples meant that numerous problems could arise for people in these relationships. For example, the report discussed how individuals in a same-sex relationship were denied the same protection against domestic violence, as barring orders could only be sought against a married partner. In many social welfare schemes, a partner could only be assessed if they were a husband or a wife, such as with the free travel pass scheme. Immigration laws for such purposes as family reunification did not apply to unmarried partners. In emergency situations a same-sex partner was not considered the next of kin and in the event of a death a same-sex partner did not have a legal right to make the funeral arrangements for their loved one. Essentially the report found that same-sex couples were denied basic protection of their relationship and of their family. However, the report did not specify how to resolve this.

The *Irish Times* acknowledged that the report 'suggests gay marriage as an option, although it cautions that there may be constitutional difficulties with this'.[31] The article further confirmed that McDowell and Bertie Ahern were not keen to consider the extension of marriage to same-sex couples as they believed this would cause constitutional concerns. This view was supported by the Attorney General, then Rory Brady, who warned the government that a change of legislation to extend marriage to same-sex couples could only be implemented through a constitutional referendum.

While the findings of the Colley Report were generally welcomed by LGBT groups, weeks later the hopes of achieving legal recognition for same-sex couples would be dashed. The outcome of the Zappone and Gilligan case concluded in December. Justice Elizabeth Dunne ultimately found in favour of the State and the findings were published on 14 December 2006. Ignoring the fact that the Irish Constitution did not include terminology excluding marriage between same-sex couples, Dunne instead looked to the recently updated Civil Registration Act for a definition of marriage in the Irish context. Justice Dunne did not engage with the discrimination argument and expressed her concern for the 'welfare of the children', thereby justifying that the State take a cautious approach on the issue. The court found insufficient evidence of any 'emerging consensus' which would support displacement of the opposite-sex rule and it pointed to the limited number of jurisdictions in which the ban on marriage for same-sex couples had been lifted. In particular, Justice Dunne took the definition of marriage contained in Ireland's Civil Registration Act 2004 which defines marriage as being between a man and a woman as an indication of the 'prevailing view' as to the definition of marriage.

Although they lost the case against the Revenue Commissioners, Zappone and Gilligan inspired an open debate on the issue of marriage for same-sex couples in Ireland. They brought the LGBT community together in support of one key issue and garnered backing from the wider community across Ireland. In her summing up of the case Justice Dunne recognised that same-sex couples faced difficulties by lack of legal recognition. She reflected that 'it is to be hoped that the legislative changes to ameliorate these difficulties will not be long in coming'. But concluded that 'ultimately, it is for the legislature to determine the extent to which such changes should be made'.[32]

## Notes

1   Ann Louise Gilligan and Katherine Zappone, *Our Lives Out Loud: In pursuit of justice and equality*, Dublin, 2008, p. 227.

2   In Chris Robson's obituary, Kieran Rose of GLEN described him as 'a huge force for wide-ranging social progress and the achievement of civil rights in Ireland over more than thirty years'; 'Tributes paid after death of LGBT and civil rights activist', *The Journal* (25 March 2013).

3   Katherine Zappone, 'In pursuit of marriage equality in Ireland: A narrative and theoretical reflection', *Equal Rights Review*, 10 (2013), 113.

4   In 2007 Bacik was elected as an independent Senator in the University of Dublin constituency.

5   Gilligan and Zappone, *Our Lives Out Loud*, p. 233.

6   Ibid., p. 253.

7   Ibid., pp. 256–7.

8   See 'History of the KAL case', Marriage Equality website, available at: www.marriagequality.ie/justlove/aboutcase/history.html (accessed 8 December 2014).

9   See the Atlantic Philanthropies website, available at: www.atlanticphilanthropies.org/grant/kal-advocacy-initiative (accessed 10 November 2014).

10  Ibid.

11  Civil Partnership Bill 2004 [Seanad], Bill Number 54 of 2004, sponsored by Senator David Norris.

12  'Civil Partnership Bill 2004: Second stage, Seanad Éireann', *Parliamentary Debates*, Vol. 179, No. 8(16 February 2005).

13  Ibid., p. 694.

14  GLEN, *Diversity Powering Success: The Building Sustainable Change Programme* (April 2006).

15  Ibid., p. 4.

16  Tony Grew, 'Gay rights group pays tribute to Bertie Ahern', *Pink News* (4 April 2008), available at: www.pinknews.co.uk/2008/04/04/gay-rights-group-pays-tribute-to-bertie-ahern/ (accessed 16 August 2018).

17  LGBT Network Service Providers, *LGBT Network News: Fortnightly e-newsletter*, Issue 20 (19 April 2006).

18  Michael McDowell, 'Opening Address', Conference on the Legal Status of Cohabitants and Same-Sex Couples at Royal College of Physicians of Ireland (26 May 2006).

19  Clodagh Sheehy, 'Anti-gay protesters attack McDowell', *Irish Examiner* (27 May 2006).

20  Una Mullally, *In the Name of Love: The movement for marriage equality in Ireland – an oral history*, Dublin, 2014, p. 70.

21 McDowell, 'Opening Address'.
22 Sheehy, 'Anti-gay protesters'.
23 Eoin Collins, 'High ambitions: Benchmarking ourselves against the best: The legal status of cohabitants and same-sex couples', Address at Conference on the Legal Status of Cohabitants and Same-Sex Couples, Royal College of Physicians of Ireland (26 May 2006).
24 Zappone, 'In pursuit of marriage equality in Ireland', 114–15.
25 Marriage Equality website, available at: www.marriagequality.ie/just-love/aboutcase/history.html (accessed 8 December 2014).
26 Ann O'Loughlin, 'Married lesbians affirm their love while in court', *Irish Independent* (5 October 2006); Ann O'Loughlin, 'No difference if children raised by lesbian parents', *Irish Independent* (7 October 2006).
27 Anne Colley, *Options Paper presented by the Working Group on Domestic Partnership* (November 2006), p. iv (hereafter 'Colley Report').
28 The Colley Report cited research which identified problems with gaining an accurate figure of same-sex co-habiting couples, including S. McManus, *Sexual Orientation Research Phase 1: A review of methodological approaches*, Edinburgh, 2003.
29 Colley Report, section 3.03.2, p. 15.
30 Ibid., section 3.08, p. 19.
31 Carl O'Brien, 'Improved terms for cohabitating couples proposed', *Irish Times* (23 November 2006).
32 Judgment, 'Zappone & Anor -v- Revenue Commissioners & Ors', High Court Record Number: 2004 19616 P (14 December 2006), available at: www.icj.org/wp-content/uploads/2012/07/Zappone-and-Gilligan-v.-Revenue-Commissioners-and-Others-High-Court-of-Ireland.pdf (accessed 4 July 2017).

# 3

# Civil partnership bills

On the same day that Zappone and Gilligan lost their High Court case against the Revenue Commissioners, Labour Party spokesperson on the Constitution and law reform, Brendan Howlin TD, tabled a Private Member's Civil Unions Bill in Dáil Éireann. Howlin, as an opposition TD, tabled a bill which differed from the Domestic Partnership Bill proposed by Norris in 2004. The Labour Party bill proposed to accord same-sex civil partners the same legal rights as married couples in the Irish State and this time the terms of the bill would be restricted to same-sex couples. It was a clever move to present the bill in this way; as Ivana Bacik pointed out, 'Private Members' bills signify the change in thinking and then eventually are adopted by the government, or the principle is adopted by the government.'[1] Although this was not civil marriage, Brian Sheehan of GLEN recognised it as 'marriage in all but name in a legal consequence'.[2] After much deliberation GLEN agreed to support the Civil Unions Bill; however, it remained committed to its now ultimate goal of achieving civil marriage.

The Civil Unions Bill was debated in Dáil Éireann on 20 February 2007. On introducing the bill for debate, Deputy Howlin described how:

> many Irish citizens in stable long-term partnerships are denied legal recognition and the protections and rights of loving couples by virtue of their gender. Irish society has progressed a long way. Today, most citizens would have no difficulty in supporting the provisions of this bill and taking this major step to ensuring legal equality for all Irish citizens.[3]

Howlin had hoped that because this bill was a 'simple measure to advance equality' TDs would unite to allow it to pass to the committee stage and any issues could be dealt with at that point.[4] However, this did not come to pass. Instead the government sought a last minute amendment and proposed that the amended bill should be read in the Dáil in six months' time. This call for a six-month delay was made with the knowledge that a general election was imminent. Howlin pointed out that once the current Dáil was dissolved any bill postponed awaiting amendments would also be dissolved. He described this as a 'shameful' move by the government – a sentiment that was echoed by the then Labour Galway West TD and later President of Ireland, Michael D. Higgins, who called it 'cynical'.[5]

The government amendment called on members of the Dáil to beware that 'the terms of the Civil Unions Bill as presented appear to be inconsistent with the provisions of the Constitution'.[6] This referred specifically to an article in the Irish Constitution relating to marriage. At the onset of the debate, Howlin addressed this point, noting that the Civil Unions Bill would not in any way change the terms of marriage as set out in the Constitution. Rather, the bill would provide for equal recognition of same-sex unions. The focus on the Constitution would become the central issue in the legal and political debate surrounding the introduction of civil partnerships and later the extension of civil marriage to same-sex couples in Ireland. This issue ensured that the Irish campaign would take a very different route from that in other countries. Elsewhere, the constitutionality of outlawing marriage for same-sex couples was at the heart of challenges. For example, in Ontario the gender-specific definition of marriage was challenged as being unconstitutional. In Ireland, on the other hand, the Constitution was being used to resist the introduction of marriage for same-sex couples.

The basic principles in Ireland differ immensely from other legal systems such as Canada, which has no single Constitution.[7] When the Constitution was written it was acknowledged that a system to amend the content should be established. Article 46 lays out a clear process through which the Irish Constitution can be amended. A proposal for an amendment must first be initiated in Dáil Éireann as a bill. If that bill is passed in both Houses of the Oireachtas, it must then be put to the people of Ireland for a public vote in a referendum.[8] The Constitution has of course been amended on a number of occasions, reflecting societal changes nationally and internationally. Amendments have focused on a wide range of issues, from the protection of Ireland's neutrality during World War Two, to a provision in 1972 to allow the State to become a member of the European Communities; on 17 June 1996, after a lengthy campaign, an article prohibiting divorce was deleted from the Constitution.

The Irish Constitution did not actually define marriage in gender-specific terms, which led the Revenue Commissioners to use a definition put forward by the *Oxford English Dictionary*. The reference to marriage appears in Article 41.3.1°, which asserts that 'the State pledges itself to guard with special care the institution of Marriage, on which the Family is founded, and to protect it against attack.'[9] Therefore, in the debate about the reading of the Civil Unions Bill, Deputy Howlin asked for confirmation from the government spokesperson as to how the introduction of such a bill could not be interpreted as an attack on the institution of marriage as recognised in the Constitution.

In his response, the Minister for Justice, Equality and Law Reform and then also Tánaiste, Michael McDowell, read the particulars of the amendment sought. The amendment sought an affirmation 'that any legislative reform in this area must be fully consistent with the provisions of the Constitution and in particular the State's constitutional duty to protect with special care the institution of marriage'.[10] However, McDowell did not offer any further discussion on how the Civil Unions Bill could contravene these provisions. McDowell also advised that it was in the interests of the Dáil to await the appeal case then pending on the issue. This referred to a resolve by Zappone and Gilligan to appeal the High Court decision on their case against the Revenue Commissioners. The women were not dissuaded by the decision of Justice Dunne and sought an appeal in the Supreme Court. This move had even more serious financial ramifications and they were again supported in their cause by Atlantic Philanthropies, which granted them €285,000 to aid with their Supreme Court challenge.

In his conclusion, McDowell was adamant that the government was dedicated to finding a resolution to protect the interests of same-sex co-habiting couples, as sought by the Colley Report. McDowell insisted that the government was not voting against the bill but that they wanted to establish a more coherent approach to civil partnerships. This was met with heated debate in the Dáil chamber, as it was acknowledged that McDowell was effectively killing the Civil Unions Bill. Howlin was indeed correct with his assertions and the Civil Unions Bill 2006 fell when the Dáil was dissolved in May 2007.

A new government was formed in June 2007, comprising Fianna Fáil, the Green Party and the Progressive Democrats. McDowell was then leader of the Progressive Democrats, a position from which he was forced to resign when he lost his seat in that election. The Labour Party remained in opposition to government and was now even more committed to introducing a legal recognition for civil partnerships in Ireland. In the 2007 manifesto, the then party leader, Pat Rabbitte, established the Labour Party's commitment 'to bring about constitutional change to provide for full equality between heterosexual and homosexual couples'. In a section entitled 'achieving full citizenship for all', a sub-section on gay rights committed to reintroduce a Civil Unions Bill to the Dáil and to ensure that 'the same rules that apply to marriage will apply to civil unions'.[11]

On 31 October 2007, Brendan Howlin again tabled a motion to introduce the same Civil Unions Bill 2006, with what he described as 'a feeling of *déjà vu*'.[12] In his introduction, Howlin was scathing of the outgoing government, which he maintained 'contrived to ensure that this bill was killed'.[13] However, he pointed out that during the Dáil debate in February 'members from all sides who contributed and spoke in favour of its provisions paid lip service to the notion of equality and stated the time for action was now. I believe now as I did then that the majority of Members support this equality measure. Therefore, it is time for them to stop mouthing about equality and to legislate for it.'[14] The recommendations of the Colley Report to introduce civil partnerships for same-sex couples which would not compete with marriage became a central issue in this debate.[15] Howlin was supported in his call by his Labour colleague Liz McManus and Sinn Féin TD, Aengus Ó Snodaigh. Sandra Irwin-Gowran, Director of Education Policy at GLEN, described how the public gallery in the Dáil was crowded that evening as people became very emotional during the debate.[16]

The bill was eventually opposed by the government. Journalist Stephen Collins clarified that this was on the grounds that it was 'contrary to the explicit recognition given to the family based on marriage in the Constitution'.[17] Brian Lenihan, then Minister for Justice, Equality and Law Reform, followed advice from the Attorney General, claiming that legislating for any other type of marriage would contravene Article 41.3.1 of the Constitution and was therefore 'constitutionally unsound'.[18] In an 'Agreed Programme for Government 2007–2012', the leaders of the three government parties committed to 'full equality for all in our society', which would be achieved partly by the introduction of 'Civil Partnerships at the earliest possible date in the lifetime of the Government'.[19] In his closing remarks on the Civil Unions Bill, Lenihan referred to the government's commitment and undertook to publish a bill relating to civil partnerships in 2008. The date was later set for publication of the bill by 31 March 2008.

While Howlin's private member's bill was being defeated inside Dáil Éireann, Labour LGBT held a vigil outside the gates of government buildings which attracted a large crowd of attendees. The attendees of the candlelit vigil were disheartened by yet another government defeat of the proposed Labour bill. The idea of holding a quiet vigil infuriated a group of activists including Annie Hanlon, Lisa Connell and Eloise McInerney, who resolved to form a more vocal pressure group to demand legislation for civil marriage. Thus LGBT Noise was founded; the name of the group signifying the more vocal approach that would be taken. The core founders made contact with Gilligan and Zappone, who supported this new initiative. The group held its first official protest on the streets of Dublin in December 2007. Members of Noise joined with Dublin's lesbian and gay choir, Gloria, where they staged a Christmas carol demonstration to bring the issue of civil marriage to public attention. In an interview with the *Irish Examiner*, Hanlon said: 'the purpose of this event is to raise awareness of the urgent need to provide protection and equality of status for gay couples; although the Government's overdue and vague proposal for a "civil partnership" scheme may alleviate some of the hardships faced by gay couples, it will not address the core issue, that of equality.'[20] This group comprised mainly young, vibrant activists and they proactively sought out new members. The group would grow over the coming months and add a new dimension to the forthcoming campaign for the extension of civil marriage to same-sex couples.

The culmination of the high-profile KAL case, the inclusion of LGBT rights in political party manifestos and the introduction of various civil partnership bills into Dáil Éireann raised public awareness about the need for legal recognition for same-sex couples. By the beginning of 2008 the focus of the KAL Advocacy Initiative, established to support the Zappone and Gilligan case against the Revenue Commissioners, was advancing beyond this single case. Their High Court case raised awareness of the issue far beyond what was initially expected. More than that, the way that Zappone and Gilligan presented themselves at court and to the media won the support of many Irish people. For perhaps the first time in Ireland, the public were presented with a loving, long-term, committed same-sex relationship in positive terms and many people, regardless of their sexuality, could relate to this. The women simply wanted their relationship to be acknowledged and protected in the same way as those of their heterosexual counterparts.

That year the KAL Advocacy Initiative developed into Marriage Equality, describing itself as 'a not for profit, national, single issue, grassroots advocacy organisation whose goal is to achieve equality for lesbian, gay, bisexual and transgender (LGBT) people in Ireland through the extension of civil marriage rights to same-sex couples'.[21] Even before the official launch of this new initiative, Board members of Marriage Equality and a long-term couple, Linda Cullen and Feargha Ní Bhroin appeared on the national RTÉ radio programme, *Today with Pat Kenny*, along with another couple, Paul Kenny and Mark McCarran. The two couples discussed how their relationships should be treated and viewed as equal in Irish society, which could only happen with the extension of civil marriage to same-sex couples. The programme aired on Valentine's Day, emphasising how romantic love is not restricted to heterosexual people. The programme was an early indication of how Marriage Equality would employ the stories of couples to show the personal side of this debate. Zappone and Gilligan had successfully garnered support across the country in this way and it was hoped that introducing personal stories to the public would shift this debate from a political and legal one to a real-life issue.

Marriage Equality was officially launched on 18 February 2008 at the Mansion House in Dublin by its founding Chairpersons, Gráinne Healy and Denise Charlton. Healy addressed a packed room to introduce Marriage Equality and described their single goal in clear terms. She announced that they sought 'the provision of equality for gay and lesbian people in Ireland by providing access to civil marriage'.[22] In a press release the day before the launch, Healy had already referred to the, still awaited, government civil partnership bill, affirming Marriage Equality's belief that 'people see immediately that civil partnership confers fewer rights, is a separate institution and is essentially unequal and discriminatory ... It is a pity the legislators who represent them continue to fail to see this.'[23]

The well-attended launch was a success in terms of raising visibility and in gaining further support for the campaign. The event also launched what was to become the trademark strategy of the organisation in the years ahead. The personal stories of same-sex couples were presented by a lesbian couple, Niamh and Jessica, and gay couple, Paul and Mark, who had appeared on the *Today with Pat Kenny* radio programme. The couples told the stories of their relationship and explained their need for protection and recognition of these relationships through civil marriage. Paul Kenny described how he was in a three-year committed relationship with Mark and 'the issue of same-sex marriage is really a matter of respect. We are in a relationship and we are contributing to society, not just as individuals but also as a couple and I feel our relationship should be respected and acknowledged by both the Government and society.'[24] This aim was supported by the Green Party, then a minor government partner. TD Ciarán Cuffe spoke at the launch, assuring attendees that his party would pressure its majority government partner Fianna Fáil to introduce civil marriage for same-sex couples. However, Cuffe noted that, as it stood, Fianna Fáil did not support this move and the government breakdown was thus 6 in favour and 78 opposed to extending civil marriage.[25] When later questioned on this, the Taoiseach, Bertie Ahern, would not comment on Cuffe's assertion.[26]

Other speakers included Moninne Griffith, who would go on to become the Director of Marriage Equality. Griffith brought with her not only key organisational skills to manage a vibrant campaign but was also a trained solicitor. This legal background proved to be an essential component when negotiating the legalities of introducing civil marriage. The Marriage Equality team had by then been put in place, with Kirsten Foster handling communications and Dawn Quinn as administrator. The communication, engagement and media presence of this organisation would become an essential and impressive part of its activities. The following year, Andrew Hyland, who had worked as a consultant in communications for Marriage Equality, joined the team as a Co-director with Griffith. Together Griffith and Hyland brought this campaign to the very heart of the LGBT community, generating a much-needed mobilisation of volunteers which essentially became a mass movement across Ireland.

Atlantic Philanthropies, which had funded the KAL Advocacy Initiative with €285,000 in 2007 to advance the equality of same-sex co-habiting couples, continued with its commitment to this cause. When Marriage Equality was founded, Atlantic initially granted it €400,000. This funding was followed by a further €250,000 granted in 2010 and €120,000 the following year. Atlantic Philanthropies remained committed to what was described in an independent review as supporting 'equality and visibility for lesbian, gay, bisexual, and transgender (LGBT) people in Ireland'.[27] Towards this end, Atlantic made regular and large grants to three other LGBT organisations from 2004–13: GLEN, Transgender Equality Network Ireland (TENI) and LGBT Diversity, a countrywide project to strengthen LGBT groups at local and national level. Atlantic was now also committed to helping introduce civil marriage for same-sex couples rather than the watered down version of civil partnerships. The funding was an essential support for Marriage Equality but the group was also under pressure to fundraise to match some of the grant money. Additionally, Atlantic was not in a position to continue funding Marriage Equality after 2011 and this had serious implications for the organisation at a crucial time.

Marriage Equality was launched in the midst of the main civil partnership debates and established only months before the government's scheme was announced by Minister Ahern, yet the organisation managed to amass an impressive media presence on the topic. The main thrust of Marriage Equality's campaign at this time was to inform the public as to how civil partnership fell short of marriage in the most fundamental of ways – a point the *Irish Independent* echoed with the headline 'Civil Partnership Bill to fall short of groups' demands', a headline which was repeated three days later in the *Irish Examiner*.[28] Tabloid newspapers also responded favourably, publishing data as hard proof that the Irish people were in support of civil marriage for same-sex couples. The *Irish Daily Mirror* maintained that 58 per cent of its readers supported 'gay marriage'.[29] As well as reporting the views of the newly established Marriage Equality, news sites were awash with positive opinion pieces.[30]

The positive and consistent media presence of Marriage Equality was part of a well-orchestrated strategy designed not only by the staff members but also by a committed Board of Directors. As with any other voluntary organisation, Board members varied over the years. Marriage Equality sought Board members from a diverse range of backgrounds with experience of equality, feminist and social campaigning together with professional experience that would complement the needs of the organisation. The final list of Board members included Gráinne Healy as Chairperson; a feminist activist with a high profile of campaigning for women's rights, she had previously chaired numerous agencies including the National Women's Council of Ireland and was a ministerial appointee to the Board of the Equality Authority and the Women's Health Council, among other key roles. The Deputy Chair, Orla Howard, came from a marketing background and had a number of years' experience from her involvement with the NLGF. Other Board members, including Olivia McEvoy and Ailbhe Smyth, also came from the ranks of the NLGF and had amassed well-earned respect in LGBT quarters.

Darina Brennan, an executive chef, recognised as an outstanding business person when she was awarded Business Person of the Year in 2010, was able to input her business strategy skills. Other Board members brought much needed legal expertise, such as Judy Walsh, a lecturer in equality studies and Director of Graduate Programmes at the School of Social Justice at University College Dublin. Justine Quinn, a barrister and later lecturer in law had a speciality in constitutional and European law, and Anna McCarthy, organiser of LGBT Noise, was also a solicitor. Carol Armstrong, a steadfast volunteer from the foundation of Marriage Equality, along with Ronan Farren, a public affairs consultant, and Ross Golden-Bannon, a political commentator, completed the Board of Directors.

The Board members were particularly impressive and held personal commitments to the advancement of the Marriage Equality cause. Many of the Board told their own personal stories to the media about their same-sex relationships and families in order to personalise the campaign. Other members over the years included co-founder Denise Charlton, a steadfast human rights activist, former Director of Women's Aid and then CEO of the Immigrant Council of Ireland, who had successfully brought what were viewed as taboo issues, such as domestic violence, into a public arena to be addressed. The financial and organisational skills of Paula Fagan, a feminist activist, trained accountant and national co-ordinator of the LGBT helpline, became central to the campaign.

Both Ann Louise Gilligan and Katherine Zappone had originally hoped that others would join them in their cause and therefore they were instantly committed to Marriage Equality as Board members. Gilligan acknowledged that 'for a social movement to really have the educational change of consciousness in a society to really happen, it has to grow beyond two people'.[31] Deirdre Hannigan, who was involved with Zappone and Gilligan's Shanty Education and Training Centre, also joined the Board members. Linda Cullen, an experienced programme maker and co-owner of television production company Coco Television, became a Board member and her skills would be effectively applied to get the Marriage Equality message to a mainstream audience. Feargha Ní Bhroin, a communications studies teacher, among her roles addressed the feminist concern with the institution of marriage in a focused research paper published by Marriage Equality.[32] Other Board members over the years included Patrick Lynch, also of the NLGF Board, Kieran O'Brien of UNICEF Ireland and Clare O'Connell whose contributions included one of the most passionate inputs to the Constitutional Convention in 2013. Fianna Fáil's Olive Braiden, an equality rights campaigner, and Chris Robson, co-founder of GLEN, who had originally been working with David Norris on his Domestic Partnership Bill, also made up the Board.

## Notes

1 Mullally, *In the Name of Love*, p. 79.
2 Ibid., p. 78.
3 Dáil Éireann, 'Civil Unions Bill 2006: Second stage', *Dáil Éireann Debate*, Vol. 631, No. 6 (20 February 2007).
4 Ibid.
5 Ibid.
6 Ibid.
7 See Government of Canada, Department of Justice website, available at: www.justice.gc.ca/eng/csj-sjc/just/05.html (accessed 8 December 2014).
8 Republic of Ireland, *Bunreacht Na hÉireann, Constitution of Ireland*, Dublin, [1937] 2012, p. 178.

 9  Ibid., p. 162.
10  Dáil Éireann, 'Civil Unions Bill 2006: Second stage'.
11  Labour Party, *The Fair Society*, Labour Party Manifesto, 2007, p. 59.
12  Dáil Éireann, 'Civil Unions Bill 2006: Restoration to order paper', *Dáil Éireann Debate*, Vol. 640, No. 4 (31 October 2007).
13  Ibid.
14  Ibid.
15  Ibid.
16  Mullally, *In the Name of Love*, p. 79.
17  Stephen Collins, 'Same-sex couples to get legal recognition next year', *Irish Times* (1 November 2007).
18  Ibid.
19  Bertie Ahern, Trevor Sargent and Mary Harney, *Programme for Government 2007–2012*, Dublin, June 2007.
20  Conor Ryan, 'Campaign for same-sex marriage takes to the streets', *Irish Examiner* (15 December 2007).
21  Marriage Equality website, available at: www.marriagequality.ie/about/history.html (accessed 8 July 2016).
22  Gráinne Healy, 'We deserve equality: Marriage Equality Co-chair tells launch audience', press release, Marriage Equality (19 February 2008).
23  Gráinne Healy, 'Change the law first, not the Constitution says Marriage Equality', press release, Marriage Equality (17 February 2008).
24  Steven Carroll, 'Call for full equality by same-sex couple', *Irish Times* (19 February 2008).
25  Steven Carroll, 'Greens seek support for same-sex marriage', *Irish Times* (19 February 2008).
26  'Civil Partnership Bill "lacks support"', *Irish Independent* (20 February 2008).
27  Barbary Cook and Rebecca Subar, *Catalysing LGBT Equality and Visibility in Ireland: A review of LGBT cluster grants, 2004–2013* (2014), p. 1.
28  'Civil Partnership Bill to fall short of groups' demands', *Irish Independent* (1 April 2008); Tom Crosbie, 'Civil Partnership Bill to fall short of groups' demands', *Irish Examiner* (4 April 2008).
29  Demelza de Burca, '58% back gay marriage', *Irish Daily Mirror* (1 April 2008).
30  Sarah Neville, 'Half of us say gays should be allowed to get married', *Irish Independent* (1 April 208).
31  Mullally, *In the Name of Love*, p. 90.
32  Feargha Ní Bhroin, *Feminism and the Same-Sex Marriage Debate* (April 2009).

# 4

# Marriage Equality:
# A new direction

Recently formed Marriage Equality had a mammoth task ahead to shift the public and political focus from civil partnerships to civil marriage. The organisation advocated through a developed approach employing four inter-connected strategies.[1] The first strategy, which was to become the most noticeable aspect of the campaign, was communications. The aim here was to improve LGBT visibility and justify why same-sex couples could only achieve equality through access to civil marriage. The second strategy was political engagement. This was an intrinsic aspect to ensure that those in positions of political power would implement the changes required to introduce marriage equality. These strategies worked hand in hand with the legal aspect which focused primarily on supporting the KAL case. If Zappone and Gilligan successfully had their marriage recognised in Ireland this would set a precedent through which other similar marriages could be recognised. The final strategy was mobilisation in order to 'engage with law makers on a grass roots level to ensure that LGBT community and the general public visit their local representatives to ensure demonstrated support for change from the public, and that public representatives are made aware of this'.[2]

In order to develop a clear and focused approach, the group looked to activists in other countries that had succeeded in introducing civil marriage for same-sex couples. One of the most successful campaigns had been led by Marc Solomon, who became a central figure in the fight to retain equal marriage for same-sex couples in Massachusetts. Marriage for same-sex couples was legalised in May 2004 in the state, following a Supreme Judicial Court ruling which held that it was unconstitutional not to extend civil marriage to all.[3] Solomon later became Political Director of MassEquality and managed to defeat a constitutional amendment in June 2007 which would overturn the legislation allowing same-sex couples to marry. This was a high-profile campaign which, if lost, could have had disastrous implications for marriage equality across the United States. After such a successful campaign Solomon went on to overturn an antiquated 1913 law in Massachusetts which outlawed same-sex couples from other states marrying there. In 2009, Solomon joined Equality California, leading campaigns there.

Ultimately, Solomon was instrumental in achieving civil marriage for same-sex couples in numerous states across America as the national Campaign Director of Freedom to Marry. Solomon has since published his account of these campaigns.[4] Zappone and Gilligan had made contact with MassEquality back in 2005 and they contacted Solomon about the new organisation of Marriage Equality in Ireland. Solomon was happy to provide guidance and advice, and he visited Dublin where he initially met with Zappone, Gilligan, Griffith and Farren. He offered advice on how to create a marriage equality campaign using the experience of his most recent campaign in Massachusetts.[5] Charlton described how Solomon was 'kind of the catalyst for Marriage Equality, and being very clear on the strands we wanted to do, which were legal, mobilisation, communication'.[6] More than this, Solomon was 'uncompromising in his position ... which was "this is equality, anything less isn't"'.[7]

This was the approach adopted from the outset by Marriage Equality – that only civil marriage would offer equality for same-sex couples. This approach did cause an initial rift between Irish LGBT groups. GLEN had worked towards the introduction of the Civil Partnership Bill and was committed to supporting it. The fact that civil partnerships would offer long-awaited legal protection for same-sex couples meant that many people were willing to accept this. Kieran Rose of GLEN described how initially he could not understand 'how saying no to progress was going to achieve progress'.[8] Marriage Equality, on the other hand, considered that the bill would place same-sex co-habiting couples in an inferior position, legally and within the wider community.

The group commissioned a position paper to introduce the public to the stance taken by Marriage Equality, the report being introduced at the launch event in the Mansion House. Simply entitled, *Making the Case for Marriage Equality*, it addressed, in unblemished terms, why civil marriage was the only possible way to grant full equality to lesbian and gay couples.[9] In the foreword, Judy Walsh stressed how legislating 'for civil partnership is to ascribe second-class citizenship to gay and lesbian people'.[10] The main position was established in the report by its author, Jane Pillinger:

> Having the right to a civil marriage is about giving lesbian and gay couples access to equality in Ireland. Anything less than that undermines equality for lesbians and gay men and is a denial of their relationships and parenting roles ... These rights are important to how lesbian and gay relationships are valued at a societal level. Marriage also provides certain social, material and familial protections that are currently not given to lesbian and gay couples and families in Ireland.
>
> Marriage equality means that everyone can be treated equally in the family and in marriage, irrespective of their sexual orientation. Giving rights to civil marriage is also a reflection of the increasing diversity of families in Ireland today, and the importance of giving respect and recognition to the validity, dignity and rights of lesbian and gay couples and families. This is not only important to how society is seen to value and affirm lesbian and gay relationships, but also to ensuring that everyone has the right to make choices about their own personal relationships, including the right to marry.
>
> Marriage equality is about giving equal rights to marriage for lesbian and gay couples on the basis that lesbian and gay people and heterosexual people are equal in the law.[11]

This report was a landmark one in that it was the first dedicated report to address why the LGBT community in Ireland deserved full marriage rights, equal to those of their heterosexual counterparts, rather than be restricted to civil partnerships. The fact that same-sex co-habiting couples had been denied any form of legal protection of their relationship in the form of State benefits meant that, for many, civil partnerships would offer welcome entitlements for the first time in Ireland. Marriage Equality needed to get a clear message across, first to the LGBT community and then to the wider community, that civil partnerships were not offering equality.

In *Making the Case for Marriage Equality in Ireland*, the main areas in which same-sex couples would be denied equal rights were established. The report broadly specified the differences for partnerships as opposed to marriage in:

> Social welfare; taxation; life insurance, pensions and benefits such as
> spousal and survivor social security benefits; rights linked to inher-
> itance and property; maintenance; rights associated with housing
> and the family home; employee related benefits in cash or in kind in
> areas such as education, transport, health insurance etc; parental leave
> and *force majeure* leave; rights of next-of-kin in life damaging and life
> threatening decisions; court cases and testifying against a partner; chil-
> dren and rights to parenthood; adoption and fostering; immigration
> and residence.[12]

In all of these areas, marriage was protected by the Constitution and
recognised by law and therefore all State services as well as public and
private sector employers. Civil partnerships would not benefit from
the same legal or constitutional protections across the board.

Another key part of the Marriage Equality campaign was introduced at the launch event: the 'Out to Your TD campaign'. This
involved a simple but highly effective tactic which was based on
models in the USA and Spain where same-sex couples lobbied their
local representatives to change the law relating to civil marriage. The
idea was based on the fact that often politicians are unaware of issues
which affect their constituents. In this instance it was very likely
that many local TDs and Senators were not aware of the number of
co-habiting same-sex couples in their constituencies and indeed the
number of those families which had children. This was highlighted
during the Dáil debate on Howlin's Civil Unions Bill in November
2007, when Fianna Fáil TD Martin Mansergh noted that 'while,
like all Deputies, I have received a number of messages urging me
to support the Labour party's bill, it is not a matter that I can recall
being raised with me, face to face, in my constituency from any angle,
either for or against'.[13] Therefore, Marriage Equality directed people
to follow five simple steps in order to ensure that local politicians
were aware of the scale of inequality that gay and lesbian couples
were living with on a daily basis. The instructions to get involved
with this campaign were posted on Marriage Equality's website and
distributed on leaflets, and volunteers emailed and phoned people on
contact lists to direct them to follow this simple procedure:

> Step 1 – Find out who your local TDs or Senators are [a clickable map
> was made available online for this] and make an appointment to visit
> all of them.

Step 2 – Contact Marriage Equality beforehand for support and info about what you might say and the views of the politicians you are visiting.

Step 3 – Visit TDs, tell your stories – how being banned from Civil Marriage impacts on your everyday life, or the lives of people you care about.

Step 4 – Encourage friends and family to do the same.

Step 5 – Contact us and let us know what your TDs said so we can keep track of their attitudes and/or support.[14]

In addition to the basic routes to engage people in the campaign action, supporters also organised meetings at their homes, inviting friends and family along to encourage them to contact their local TD. Thousands of people supported this plan and this was not restricted to the gay and lesbian community. Parents, friends and supporters of LGBT people made appointments to see their local politicians and demanded that they support calls for the introduction of civil marriage equality.

In addition, Marriage Equality ensured that the Out to Your TD campaign received much-needed media attention. Board member Orla Howard, along with her partner Gráinne Courtney and their children, Daire and Clare O'Connell, were accompanied by an *Irish Times* journalist when they met with their local representatives on the issue. The family arranged to meet with Fine Gael's Richard Bruton and Independent TD Finian McGrath, representatives in their Dublin North Central constituency, at Leinster House. The meeting was reported by *Irish Times* journalist Róisín Ingle. The message that the children wanted to present at that meeting was simple; as summed up by Clare, 'we want to be able to say we have a real family, we don't want anyone to be able to question that. We want people to see that children of lesbian parents aren't all messed up, we are normal, we deserve the same rights as anyone else.'[15] However, this was not going to be an easy meeting with Bruton, who arrived brandishing a copy of his party's out-dated document on civil partnerships. As soon as he met with the family he announced that this is 'not my area of expertise'.[16]

Ultimately Bruton would express his view that it would be easier to introduce civil partnerships for same-sex couples rather than civil marriage. This opinion was to become the basis of many political arguments over the coming years. Bruton told the family that he believed the only way for marriage to be extended to same-sex couples would be through a constitutional referendum. This he saw as problematic because 'pursuing the constitutional route has always been very divisive [as] it would be difficult to convince the country about that, whereas civil partnership is a way of establishing something that works and then you can revisit the deeper, more philosophical issue when it's in place'.[17] This view almost echoed the position of opposition party Fianna Fáil when expressed by the Minister for Justice, Brian Lenihan, months earlier. In his address at the launch of the GLEN annual report in December 2007, Lenihan stated that it was his 'strong belief, based on sound legal advice, that gay marriage would require constitutional change and in my view a referendum on this issue at this time would be divisive and unsuccessful'.[18]

The next meeting, with Independent TD Finian McGrath, was to have a very different outcome. McGrath instantly told the family that he fully supported their call for civil marriage and offered suggestions about organising a group of TDs who could support the move in the Dáil. He offered to organise what he called a 'core group [of TDs] who support the principles of equality on the issue of marriage'.[19] This was a positive move and drove the Out to Your TD campaign further along its course.

This was an impressive week of activities for the newly formed Marriage Equality. The launch event saw a large attendance and their objectives were quoted in all of the national newspapers and across the radio waves. Their initiatives, including telling personal stories and the Out to Your TD campaign, were already well underway. This media attention and community organisation generated further interest and members began appearing on major national television programmes. The now considerable media exposure would also incite a backlash from opponents to marriage for same-sex couples. The day after the launch event, Gráinne Healy appeared on RTÉ's *Prime Time*, the most viewed national Irish current affairs programme.[20] The programme was presented by Miriam O'Callaghan and also included Margaret Gill, a bereaved mother whose daughter, Barbara, had been in a long-term relationship and had had a son with her female partner eight weeks before her tragic death. Gill's story highlighted a central issue in this debate regarding the legal protection of the children of same-sex partners, which the Civil Partnership Bill would not cover. Other guests included David Quinn, a religious and social affairs commentator and, more importantly in this instance, the Director of the Iona Institute. Members of the Iona Institute would become the most vocal opponents to the introduction of civil marriage for same-sex couples in the years to come. The Institute describe themselves as promoting 'the place of marriage and religion in society. Out [sic] starting point in debates about the family is that children deserve the love of their own mother and father whenever possible. We believe in publicily- [sic] funded denominational schools. We also promote freedom of conscience and religion.'[21]

Days after the programme aired, Healy, along with Board members Orla Howard and Patrick Lynch, participated in a live debate with members of the Iona Institute on RTÉ Radio One's *Spirit Moves*. The media seemed awash with positive stories, and the morning after co-founder of Marriage Equality, Denise Charlton and her partner and fellow Board member, Paula Fagan, wrote an article for the *Irish Times* entitled 'Time to open civil marriage to lesbian and gay couples'. The couple were not only in a long-term partnership but also parents. They shared their personal story and explained how not having the protection of civil marriage negatively impacted on the rights of their son. They explained in the article that 'our son's non-biological mother doesn't have any rights to him and, critically, from a child protection and welfare point of view, he does not have rights to the woman he recognises as his mother. Instead, his human right to both of his parents is at the arbitrary discretion of a society which knows very little about him or his family.'[22]

Such personal stories brought strong reactions from the general public who, often for the first time, were introduced to the reality that there were other family set-ups just as valuable as their own. More importantly, it was now evident that these families were not cherished by the law or constitutional protection in Ireland. This was a major strand of the Marriage Equality campaign and it was recognised as a powerful tool even by their opponents. These personal stories generated instant concern in organisations such as the Iona Institute. Member and co-founder, Patricia Casey, responded to Charlton and Fagan's interview in the letter pages of the *Irish Times*. Casey warned that there was 'a real danger that this debate is going to be led by emotion. It must instead be led by reason and a calm consideration of the facts.'[23] If anything, this response was a measure of the campaign's early success, which clearly concerned opponent groups.

Also a measure of success was the fact that readers attacked Casey's letter. A psychiatrist based in Michigan, USA, Brian Connolly, replied through the letter pages to strongly refute Casey's claims that children should be raised by heterosexual couples. Joan Courtney and Frances Byrne, representing OPEN, a lone-parent advocacy organisation, also wrote to express their support of the Marriage Equality cause, noting that 'there is genuine emotion among families in Ireland who do not "fit" the recognised norm. An authentic debate on any topic should give voice to those whose everyday lives are affected by the issue.'[24] This debate regarding same-sex couples parenting their own children would continue in the letter pages of the *Irish Times* for weeks to come. On 4 March, Healy responded, citing research done by numerous highly respected organisations including 'the American Psychological Association; the Australian Psychological Association; the Canadian Psychological Association; the Royal College of Psychiatrists (UK); the National Association of Social Workers (USA); and the American Psychiatric Association ... all of which state that children raised by gay and lesbian parents are in no way disadvantaged'.[25]

One of the most powerful stories came from Margaret Gill, who had appeared with Healy on *Prime Time*. It was a tragic case. Her daughter, Barbara Gill, was in a thirteen-year relationship with Ruth O'Dwyer. The couple had a son together. When the couple's son, Stephen, was just eight weeks old Barbara met with a fatal accident while on her way to work. She was knocked off her bicycle by a skip truck and died hours later. As Barbara was the non-biological parent of Stephen he had no next-of-kin inheritance rights to her estate; neither did her life partner as they were denied the right to marry. While Barbara and Ruth had re-written their wills, they had not signed them by the time the tragedy occurred. Barbara's parents inherited their daughter's estate but they understood that her partner and her child were the rightful benefactors. According to Irish law Barbara's parents would have to gift the estate and therefore be subject to exorbitant tax. Barbara had been a supporter of the marriage equality campaign. In fact, she had been one of the first people to contact Sandra Irwin-Gowran to take part in GLEN's 'Share Your Story' drive. The initiative involved locating people in same-sex relationships who would share their stories and 'talk about the impact legal recognition would have on their lives'.[26] At that stage the Gill family could not have envisaged how significant the issue of marriage equality would be to them.

Margaret Gill appeared on *Prime Time* to tell her story and show how her daughter's family had been affected because civil marriage was not available to same-sex couples. Additionally, she explained her upset that she was not even legally acknowledged as a relation to Stephen, who was her grandson. This story was so powerful that it became a key argument in a Seanad motion days later. On 28 February, Senators David Norris and Ivana Bacik tabled a motion to introduce civil marriage for same-sex couples. Norris introduced the motion, relating it to decriminalisation of homosexuality in 1993. At which time Norris noted that:

> the then Minister for Justice indicated that clear factual and cogent arguments rather than prejudice would be required to support discrimination in law against any Irish citizen, and in the light of the reports of various think tanks and Commissions but most particularly the Colley Report, urges the Government at last to introduce full equality under the law for gay citizens of Ireland including access to civil marriage.[27]

In his response, Minister Lenihan referred to the Civil Partnership Bill being prepared by the government which, he said, would 'provide a statutory scheme from which same-sex couples who choose to register their partnerships will derive extensive rights and protections. This scheme will build on the Colley options paper and the Law Reform Commission report on cohabitants.'[28] He reiterated his view that marriage for same-sex couples would be unconstitutional.

During the heated debate that followed Senator Rónán Mullen referred to the current media presence on the topic and derided the use of personal stories. He described it as 'disingenuous to take individual cases in which justice must be done, regardless of whether they pertain to inheritance in scenarios in which people who are mutually dependent find themselves in difficulties or to children who are not getting their rights'.[29] Senator Frances Fitzgerald responded by attesting that 'individual cases bring home to us the reality of people's lives' and specifically mentioned Margaret Gill's story. The Norris and Bacik motion was defeated but this was a welcome debate on civil marriage as opposed to civil partnership in the Seanad.

Margaret Gill's story continued to cause outrage among a broad section of the Irish population. Gill became an important part of the Marriage Equality campaign and she was invited to speak on *The Late Late Show* on 28 March. Her personal story and the stories of so many others were now being presented regularly through media outlets. This generated great indignation from opponents to marriage equality, especially from other religious-based groups including the Family and Media Association (FMA). The FMA describes its aims as twofold: 'to promote greater understanding and appreciation of Christian values in the media with particular reference to Catholic teaching and to promote public understanding of the functioning and power of the media and, in so doing, foster high standards of honesty, decency, fairness, objectivity, impartiality and truthfulness'.[30] Part of the way the FMA strives to achieve its objectives is by lodging complaints about what it considers 'unbalanced' or 'misleading' programmes. After monitoring the media relating to Marriage Equality in the week of the group's launch, FMA member Kevin Dolan submitted a complaint through the official channels of the Broadcasting Complaints Commission. In his complaint Dolan referred specifically to the *Prime Time* programme aired on 19 February. He maintained that this programme was an infringement of 'fairness, objectivity & impartiality in current affairs' and to 'objectivity & impartiality in news and current affairs in RTÉ published matter'.[31] This was just the beginning of what would become an ongoing battle with the media surrounding Marriage Equality's campaign.

### Notes

1 As described by independent evaluators O'Carroll Associates and Hibernian Consulting. Íde O'Carroll and Finbar McDonnell, *Marriage Equality: Case study final version*, Dublin, 2010.
2 Ibid., p. 6.
3 *Goodridge v. Department of Public Health (Massachusetts 2003)* was launched by seven couples represented by GLAD.
4 Marc Solomon, *Winning Marriage: The inside story of how same-sex couples took on the politicians and pundits—and won*, New England, 2014.
5 Mullally, *In the Name of Love*, p. 90.
6 Ibid., p. 90.
7 Ibid., p. 91.
8 Ibid., p. 97.
9 Jane Pillinger, *Making the Case for Marriage Equality in Ireland: Marriage Equality position paper* (February 2008).

10 Ibid., p. 3.
11 Ibid., p. 9.
12 Ibid., p. 11.
13 Dáil Éireann, 'Private Members' Business – Civil Unions Bill 2006: Restoration to order paper (resumed)', *Dáil Éireann Debate*, Vol. 640, No. 51 (1 November 2007).
14 Marriage Equality, 'Out to Your TD Campaign', available at: www.marriagequality.ie (accessed 17 July 2016).
15 Róisín Ingle, 'Families come out for gay marriage', *Irish Times* (16 February 2008).
16 Ibid.
17 Ibid.
18 Carl O'Brien, 'Lenihan rules out "divisive" referendum on gay marriage', *Irish Times* (5 December 2007).
19 Ingle, 'Families come out for gay marriage'.
20 *Prime Time* (19 February 2016).
21 The Iona Institute website, available at: www.ionainstitute.ie/about-the-iona-institute/ (accessed 18 July 2016).
22 'Time to open civil marriage to lesbian and gay couples', *Irish Times* (25 February 2008).
23 'Debate on same-sex marriage', *Irish Times* (28 February 2008).
24 Ibid.
25 *Irish Times* (4 March 2008).
26 Mullally, *In the Name of Love*, p. 111.
27 'Civil Marriage Motion', *Seanad Éireann Debate*, Vol. 188, No. 17 (27 February 2008).
28 Ibid.
29 Ibid.
30 FMA website, available at: http://fma.ie/fma/about/ (accessed 18 July 2016).
31 Kevin Dolan, 'Complaint Form', Broadcasting Complaints Commission (20 March 2008), available at: www.metamedia.ie/complaint_prime_time_19_feb_2008_same_sex_adoption.pdf (accessed 5 September 2016).

# 5

# Political lobbying, the media and influencing public opinion

While the Marriage Equality campaign was gaining ground, the government continued working on issuing a Civil Partnership Bill but failed to reach its own March deadline date. In April 2008, the European Court of Justice ruled in favour of granting a same-sex partner pension entitlement on the death of their loved one. However, this would only apply to European countries where civil partnerships were legally recognised. This move and the release of some details relating to the government's proposed Civil Partnership Bill generated more media debate. Social affairs correspondent for the *Irish Times*, Carl O'Brien, was quick to note that while the proposed civil partnership legislation would grant same-sex couples many benefits that married couples received, this would not include the protection of children within those relationships. O'Brien pointed out that any future heads of the Civil Partnership Bill 'is unlikely to go far enough to meet demands of same-sex lobby groups who want full marriage and equality before the law for same-sex couples'.[1] The *Irish Examiner* carried the most recent opinion polls on the topic, with a Lansdowne Market Research poll showing that 84 per cent of respondents were in favour of civil marriage or civil partnerships for same-sex couples.[2] Tabloid newspapers such as the *Irish Daily Star* published positive reports, praising how 'Ireland is warming to gay marriage'.[3]

In the midst of open debate about the forthcoming Civil Partnership Bill a significant case regarding legal recognition for same-sex family units was brought before the High Court. The case involved a lesbian couple (named as P.L. and B.M. in court proceedings) who gave birth to a son through artificial insemination using sperm donated from a friend. In March 2008, one of the women was appointed to a temporary senior position as a psychiatrist in Australia and they announced their plans to leave the country for one year. The sperm donor, claiming rights as the biological father, applied to the High Court for an order to restrain the couple from removing the child from Ireland. In a landmark decision, Mr Justice John Hedigan denied the donor rights of access or guardianship; furthermore he ruled that the couple and the baby were a family unit under the European Convention on Human Rights.

The case proceeded to the Supreme Court for appeal the next year, at which time Ms Justice Susan Denham granted the donor access rights to the child as the biological father but fell short of granting him guardianship. The case highlighted the need to provide legal protection to the family unit of same-sex couples, especially in light of the final Supreme Court ruling in which Justice Denham concluded:

> The respondents do not form a de facto family in Irish law. P.L., as the mother of the child, has a natural right guaranteed by the Constitution to his custody and to look after his general care, his nurture, his physical and moral wellbeing and his education, in every respect. The child has corresponding rights as a human person to those benefits. B.M. has no legally or constitutionally recognisable family relationship with the child.[4]

The issue of legal rights for children of same-sex couples would become a central concern when the heads of a Civil Partnership Bill was released on 24 June 2008. This document outlined the government's proposed scheme to recognise the rights and duties of co-habiting couples. The government produced the outline taking into account both the recommendations of the Colley Report and the KAL legal case, which was still awaiting a Supreme Court hearing. Due to a cabinet reshuffle, Brian Lenihan was promoted to Minister for Finance and yet another Minister for Justice, Equality and Law Reform, Dermot Ahern, was then in place. The shuffle was necessary after the retirement of Bertie Ahern in May 2008. Brian Cowen succeeded as the Fianna Fáil Taoiseach with Mary Coughlan also of Fianna Fáil as Tánaiste. The placement of Dermot Ahern as Minister for Justice caused concern within LGBT quarters as 'he had not been supportive of the decriminalization of homosexuality while a member of the Dáil in 1993'.[5] However, in his publication of the proposed

Civil Partnership Bill, Ahern noted how this proposal 'represents a recognition by Government of the many forms of relationships in modern society, and an important step very particularly for same-sex couples, whose relationships have not previously been given legal recognition'.[6] Acknowledging the personal and social implications of this bill for the lives of so many, the government, then comprising Fianna Fáil, the Green Party and the Progressive Democrats, called for interested parties to examine the scheme and submit opinions.

After examination of the scheme a challenge came from an unexpected source – senior backbenchers in Fianna Fáil. Two days after the heads of the bill was published, Jim Walsh, a Fianna Fáil Senator based in Wexford, put forward a party motion against its introduction. He was supported by up to thirty unnamed Fianna Fáil TDs and Senators.[7] The objection did not gain momentum when discussed at the parliamentary party's justice committee the following week, when it was confirmed that the legislation was drawn up with the support of the Attorney General and therefore did not contravene the Constitution. The attempted opposition was described in negative terms by media sources; the *Irish Times* called it an attempt to 'deny gay couples right to register'.[8] The proposed scheme was cited in the *Irish Yearbook of International Law* that year as one which sought to 'grant gay, lesbian and bi-sexual couples in same-sex relationships the right to enter into a civil partnership. While not equated with marriage, the 2008 scheme provides a similar (though not identical) range of rights to that of marriage.'[9]

The scheme did offer a number of rights previously denied to same-sex couples, including pension entitlements, succession and immigration rights, and legislation regarding the family home. However, it fell far short of the benefits extended to married heterosexual couples, especially in its failing to provide any entitlements to children of same-sex relationships. There was instant retaliation to this omission; opposition TD Aengus Ó Snodaigh released a statement that 'his party [Sinn Féin] would like to see the legislation provide for marriage and adoption rights for same-sex couples and he will be seeking to amend the legislation accordingly when it is debated in the Dáil'.[10]

Dermot Ahern submitted the scheme of the bill to the IHRC, a government body established under the remit of the Human Rights Commission Acts. The IHRC published its considerations of the scheme in December 2008. The preface to the findings unequivocally supported the need to provide legislation which would protect the rights of same-sex committed relationships. It described 'the drafting of the scheme of the bill [as] a response to a growing recognition in Irish society of the hurt and suffering inflicted on members of the lesbian and gay communities by years, even centuries, of prejudice, discrimination and persecution'.[11]

The IHRC clearly advocated for the introduction of a system through which same-sex relationships would be protected and afforded similar legal rights to those of heterosexual couples in Ireland. In its summary, the Commission raised a number of legally binding national and international agreements which impacted on the decision of the State to introduce civil partnerships, some of which had been previously overlooked. In particular they drew attention to the Belfast / Good Friday Agreement. This Agreement, signed in 1998, specified that the Irish State was responsible for ensuring that human rights within its jurisdiction would offer 'at least an equivalent level of protection of human rights as will pertain in Northern Ireland'.[12] Under this remit, if human rights legislation were adopted in Northern Ireland, even after the introduction of the 1998 Agreement, the Irish State was bound to introduce comparable measures. The Civil Partnership Act introduced in 2004 enabled same-sex couples to legally enter into a civil partnership in Northern Ireland and therefore the Irish State was now obliged to introduce similar legislation.

Although countries within the United Kingdom – England, Scotland and Wales – had extended civil marriage to same-sex couples by the end of 2014, the issue remained contentious in Northern Ireland and the region did not follow suit. Therefore, there was no obligation for the Irish State to consider introducing civil marriage for same-sex couples under the terms of the Good Friday Agreement. In addition, the IHRC confirmed that there was no obligation to provide civil marriage under any international human rights laws.[13] However, one of the major concerns for campaigners was that civil partnerships did not offer equivalent rights to civil marriage, especially in relation to the children of such partnerships. This was addressed by the IHRC, which highlighted that the scheme failed to include any consideration for the children of same-sex relationships. In fact the scheme made no mention of such children. In this aspect they asserted that 'the best interests of the child should be the primary consideration. Children raised within a civil partnership should be treated equally with other children raised within opposite-sex relationships.'[14]

Regardless of the obvious flaws of the scheme being pointed out by opposition TDs and the IHRC, the scheme of the bill went forward. GLEN regarded civil partnerships as offering 'urgently needed protections', and supported its introduction.[15] In a report in the *Irish Times*, Kieran Rose welcomed the news, stating that 'this is a reform whose time has come. All political parties have played a role in getting us to this point and there is huge public support for change.'[16] Although it was anticipated that the bill would pass within six months and come into law by June 2009, this proved to be a much slower process.

Nearly one year to the day that the heads of the bill was produced, on 26 June 2009, Minister Dermot Ahern published the full Civil Partnership Bill. This would be the first of a three-stage process before the bill could be signed into law. The bill, entitled 'an act to provide for the registration of civil partners and for the consequences of that registration, to provide for the rights and obligations of cohabitants to provide for connected matters', was far short of the legislative changes sought by campaigners.[17] Even before the bill was published the pressure group EQUALS organised a vibrant demonstration claiming the bill sought to create a 'two tier society where gay people and their families are treated as second class citizens'.[18] Protestors chained themselves to the gates of Dáil Éireann and unfurled a rainbow flag emblazoned with the slogan 'Marriage Rights Are Equal Rights'.

Labour TD, Brendan Howlin attacked the basis of the bill, releasing a statement that 'while providing a welcome advance for the many thousands of loving same-sex couples who want to have their relationship recognised by the State to which they pay taxes, [the bill] certainly falls short in terms of this commitment to equality'.[19] Howlin was quick to point out that 'it is ironic that the Greens criticised Labour's bill for not going far enough when it was first introduced in Dáil Éireann. Now that they have arrived in Government they are content to settle for a lot less.'[20] Although disappointed by the Green Party's stance, Gráinne Healy was a little more sympathetic to the dilemma in which the party found themselves. Healy maintained a good working relationship with the party, concluding that although they were committed to achieving 'marriage equality ... once they got in [to government] they realised, "All we're going to get here [is civil partnership], so we're going to go for that." '[21]

The bill was published the day before the annual Dublin Pride parade was due to take place. In 2009 the theme was Pride and Prejudice? A record turnout, estimated at 12,500 people, took part in the parade, which culminated in a post-parade rally at Dublin civic offices. In her address to the crowd, Ailbhe Smyth of Marriage Equality, and that year's Grand Marshall, compared the bill in harsh terms to an 'apartheid system'.[22] Smyth, like many others at the rally, was angered and stated clearly that 'we are not to be insulted and humiliated, we want marriage for lesbians and gays, our goal is equality.'[23] The crowd's anger reached a height when Anna McCarthy of Noise took to the stage and ripped up a copy of the bill to riotous applause. The reaction to the bill at a Pride event was a cause for concern for members of GLEN in attendance that day. GLEN had worked at introducing the bill and Tiernan Brady described how they 'knew it wasn't everything ... but that we were utterly convinced that (a) this addressed the real need of the people now (b) this was what was politically achievable now'.[24] Rose further summed up his upset at the Pride condemnation, describing it as 'ripping up people's aspirations'.[25] However, this event marked a clear change of attitude among the general lesbian and gay community, who now appeared to support Marriage Equality's ethos that anything less than full civil marriage for same-sex couples was simply not equality.

Parade host Panti Bliss (drag persona name of Rory O'Neill) addressed this division in the LGBT community over the Civil Partnership Bill, taking to the stage to say that 'some think it is a stepping stone to full equality, some disagree and think full equality is the only thing that we can accept, all agree that the proposed bill does not go far enough ... Anyone can get married in this country except you, any soccer hooligan, any gay basher, any fascist, any murderer, any sex offender can get married, but you cannot.'[26] These sentiments echo early feminist campaigns for votes for women which, in the early twentieth century, pointed out that criminals and white slave traders could vote while women could not. After this speech Panti would become a central figure in the campaign to secure marriage equality in Ireland.[27]

After this speech, Panti also became a target of columnist Brenda Power, who attempted to demean the content of her address. Writing in the pages of the *Sunday Times* the following week, Power announced how 'it is not easy for a man to make a serious political point on the shortcomings of the new Civil Partnership Bill while he is wearing half a wedding dress and calling himself Miss Panti.'[28] Power went further in her article by attacking the behaviour and sexual identity of those present at the rally. She observed that 'homosexuals insist that their nature is an inherent, essential reality, and not a lifestyle choice. But if we were to judge by the get-up and carry-on of some of those in the Pride march last week, that's hard to believe. Some are definitely choosing to pursue a way of life that is quite alien to the majority of married heterosexual parents in this country, indeed deliberately and defiantly so.'[29] The article caused a backlash and many readers wrote letters of complaint to the *Sunday Times*. The article was just the beginning of what would become a public feud between Panti and Power.

The Pride parade brought attention to the perceived deficiencies of the Civil Partnership Bill from within the lesbian and gay community. Marriage Equality members took advantage of this new public interest, leading debates on social media, in national newspapers and across other media outlets. One of the group's most influential contributions at this time was a short film entitled *Sinead's Hand*. The film was launched at the Annual Dublin Lesbian and Gay Film Festival, on 1–3 August 2009. The film opens with Irish actor Hugh O'Connor, dressed in a smart suit to impress, calling at a man's door to ask permission for Sinead's hand in marriage. The clever turn of plot then sees O'Connor travelling the length and breadth of Ireland, through urban and rural settings, knocking on every house door to ask for permission for Sinead's hand in marriage. To the musical soundtrack of 'Ocean and Rock' by Irish artist Lisa Hannigan, the Marriage Equality message appears on screen asking, 'how would you feel if you had to ask four million people permission to get married?' The film was initiated by Marriage Equality Board member, Linda Cullen, who was inspired by an American film commissioned by Freedom to Marry called *Permission*. The film became a viral hit and brought further attention to the fact that, as noted in the final frame of the film, 'lesbians and gay men are denied access to civil marriage in Ireland'. In an interview with *Pink News*, Andrew Hyland, then

Co-director of Marriage Equality, described the media sensation, noting how 'apparently it [*Sinead's Hand*] is spreading like wildfire. People from the UK, Ireland, America and all over the world have seen it. It's one of those things that once you've seen it, it stays with you.'[30]

Campaigners retaliated further and on 9 August, Noise organised a mass protest in Dublin, calling for full civil marriage equality. An estimated five thousand people marched from City Hall to the Department of Justice. The former Director of the Equality Authority, Niall Crowley, addressed the crowd, calling the proposed civil partnership legislation 'a retrograde step, merely tolerating but not valuing diversity'.[31] This first Irish 'March for Marriage' would become an annual event in the run-up to the Marriage Equality referendum. Similar marches were being held internationally as the call for the extension of civil marriage to all became a global quest.

In the midst of heated public debates, the Civil Partnership Bill 2009 was introduced to the second stage on 3 December 2009. The bill was debated in the Dáil in January. The public outcry against the bill was recognised during these debates by Labour TD Ciaran Lynch, who affirmed that 'the gay community's aspiration was for full legal equality with their heterosexual peers, as it should be'.[32] However, Lynch maintained that he was advised by the Attorney General and his party's legal counsel that a constitutional referendum would be needed in order to extend civil marriage to same-sex couples. During the Dáil debates, protests were held outside government buildings led by the main LGBT groups. Nevertheless, the bill went forward and completed the committee stage on 27 May 2010. The bill finally passed the Dáil on 1 July 2010. Muriel Walls of GLEN described sitting in the Dáil public gallery that night surrounded by members of various LGBT groups including BelongTo, the Irish LGBT youth organisation. Wallis describes the passing of the bill as 'magical', when 'everybody just erupted in cheers, hugging'.[33]

The bill passed through Dáil Éireann without the need for a vote; it was supported unanimously. It then passed to the Upper House of the Oireachtas, Seanad Éireann, for a vote. This was a problematic stage which witnessed no less than seventy-seven proposed amendments to the bill and resulted in impassioned debate. Ivana Bacik observed that although the bill was presented by a coalition government of Fianna Fáil and the Green Party, with all parties supporting, there were a number of Fianna Fáil Senators 'strongly opposed' to it.[34] The Independent Senator Rónán Mullen also held steadfastly to his opposition. The proposed amendments caused controversy and upset as Senator David Norris explained the proposal to include what were termed ' "conscience clauses" which would allow confectioners or hairdressers or the renters of premises or the printers of stationery or florists to refuse to grant their services if they thought' a couple were gay.[35] Further proposals in the Seanad included extending the Civil Partnership Bill to include other forms of relationships such as sisters and brothers who could then avail of the same legislative protections as a committed same-sex couple. Averil Power, then political advisor to Tourism Minister Mary Hanafin, described her disbelief at such proposals. Power simply could not 'understand how people can miss the basic fact that there's a difference between an intimate loving relationship and a familial relationship or a friendship or anything else'.[36]

Eventually, on 8 July 2010, the Civil Partnership Bill was passed by the Seanad through a vote of 48 in favour and 4 against. The bill just needed one final sign of approval which it received on 19 July when it was signed by the then President of Ireland, Mary McAleese. The Civil Partnership and Certain Rights and Obligations of Cohabitants Act 2010 came into legal effect on 1 January 2011. In that first year, 536 same-sex couples obtained legal recognition of their relationships through a civil partnership ceremony. Of this number, 335 unions were between male couples and 201 between female couples. During the life of this act, which ended on the introduction of civil marriage for same-sex couples in 2015, more than two thousand same-sex couples availed of civil partnerships.[37] Linda Cullen of Marriage Equality explained that couples availed of this because they had no alternative to gain some legal recognition for their relationship. She noted that 'it's a mistake to think that the amount of people getting civilly partnered means that it's a great success. It does not. People are doing it because they really feel they have to.'[38] While there was a general feeling among the LGBT community that civil partnerships had established a two-tier relationship, there were others, including Tiernan Brady, who believed that at least the new law 'slowly created a visibility of couples, which again took it to a new level'.[39]

# Notes

1  Carl O'Brien, 'Same-sex unions to get many benefits of marriage', *Irish Times* (1 April 2008).
2  'Support for gay marriage grows', *Irish Examiner* (1 April 2008).
3  David O'Brien, 'Ireland is warming to gay marriage', *Irish Daily Star* (1 April 2008).
4  Supreme Court, 'In the matter of the Guardianship of Infants Act, 1964 and in the matter of the Family Law Act, 1995 and in the matter of the Child Abduction and Enforcement of Custody Act, 1991 and in the matter of Hugh Larkin, An Infant', Record No. 186/2008 (10 December 2009).
5  Centre for Evaluation Innovation, *Civil Partnership and Ireland: How a minority advocacy group achieved a majority*. A case study of the Gay and Lesbian Equality Network (November 2012), p. 9.
6  Department of Justice and Equality, 'Publication of Civil Partnership Bill', press release (24 June 2008).
7  Mark Hennessy, 'FF Senator leads move to deny gay couples right to register', *Irish Times* (27 June 2008).
8  Ibid.
9  Jean Allain and Siobhán Mullally (eds), *The Irish Yearbook of International Law, Volume 3*, Oxford, 2008, p. 167.
10  Aengus Ó Snodaigh, 'Government must do better than Civil Partnership Bill' (24 June 2008), Sinn Féin website, available at: www.sinnfein.ie/contents/13050 (accessed 6 July 2008).
11  Irish Human Rights Commission, *Discussion Document on the Scheme of the Civil Partnership Bill* (December 2008), p. 3.
12  Ibid., p. 23.
13  Ibid., p. 51.
14  Ibid., p. 67.
15  Healy, Sheehan and Whelan, *Ireland Says Yes*, p. 15.
16  Carl O'Brien, 'Mixed response to plans for civil unions', *Irish Times* (2 April 2008).
17  Bill Number 44 of 2009, Sponsored by Minister for Justice, Equality and Law Reform (24 June 2009) changed to Civil Partnership and Certain Rights and Obligations of Cohabitants Bill 2009.
18  'Gay rights activists chained to Dail', *Herald* (26 June 2009).
19  Statement by Brendan Howlin TD, 'Civil Partnership Bill falls short of Government commitment on equality' (26 June 2009), available at: www.labour.ie (accessed 30 August 2019).
20  Ibid.
21  Mullally, *In the Name of Love*, p. 145.

22 Genevieve Carbery, 'Dublin Pride celebrations soured by anger over Civil Partnership Bill', *Irish Times* (29 June 2009).

23 Ibid.

24 Mullally, *In the Name of Love*, p. 154.

25 Ibid., p. 155.

26 Carbery, 'Dublin Pride celebrations'.

27 See Fintan Walsh for an insightful take on the theatrics of the Marriage Equality campaign in *Queer Performance and Contemporary Ireland: Dissent and disorientation*, London, 2016.

28 Brenda Power, 'You can't trample over the wedding cake and eat it', *Sunday Times* (5 July 2009).

29 Ibid.

30 Jessica Geen, 'Video: Irish gay marriage ad becomes a surprise internet hit', *Pink News* (4 September 2009).

31 '5,000 join same-sex marriage protest', *Metro* (10 August 2009).

32 Michael O'Regan, 'Dáil debates civil unions bill', *Irish Times* (21 January 2010).

33 Mullally, *In the Name of Love*, p. 179.

34 Ibid., p. 180.

35 Ibid., p. 181.

36 Ibid., p. 182.

37 Marriages and Civil Partnerships 2011; 2012; 2013; 2014; and 2015, Central Statistics Office Ireland, available at: www.cso.ie/en/ (accessed 1 June 2017).

38 Mullally, *In the Name of Love*, p. 205.

39 Ibid., p. 205.

# 6

# Meeting the challenges of the twenty-first century

Shortly after civil partnerships came into effect the coalition government collapsed. The Green Party withdrew from government on 23
January 2011, forcing then Taoiseach, Brian Cowen, to call a general
election. This was a time ripe for political reform. Each of the main
political parties recognised a need for constitutional change, reflected
in their election manifestos. Fianna Fáil acknowledged that 'it is
absolutely clear that no significant programme of political reform
which involves amending the constitution can succeed without a real
engagement with citizens during the process of drafting proposals'
and therefore suggested a citizens' assembly.[1] Fine Gael also proposed a citizens' assembly, outlining how this would comprise up
to '100 members who will be chosen from the public to reflect the
demographic make-up of the country'.[2] Furthermore, Fine Gael proposed a Constitution Day which they committed to holding within
twelve months of assuming office. Sinn Féin proposed redrafting a
new Constitution through an all-Ireland Constitutional Forum.[3] The
idea of a new Constitution was also put forward by the Labour Party
through a system of a Constitutional Convention made up of ninety
members of ordinary citizens as well as political representatives and
people with relevant professional experience.[4] The Green Party followed this same proposal based on a process of a citizens' assembly.[5]

The general election took place on 25 February and the results
heralded a dramatic change to the Irish political landscape. Fianna
Fáil, which had been the majority party in government, lost nearly
half of its first preference votes and secured only twenty seats.
Fine Gael and the Labour Party won more seats than ever in their
respective histories. Writing in the *Irish Times*, historian Diarmaid

Ferriter described Fianna Fáil's downfall as a 'defeat on a historic scale'.[6] Fine Gael and Labour engaged in intense negotiations and formed a programme for government in March 2011. In their 'Statement of Common Purpose' the parties gloried in the results of the election. In their introduction they claimed that 'a democratic revolution took place in Ireland. Old beliefs, traditions and expectations were blown away. The stroke of a pen, in thousands of polling stations, created this political whirlwind'.[7] Yet another coalition government was formed, this time with Fine Gael as a majority partner and Labour in minority. With the Labour Party now in government, activists were hopeful that the drive towards marriage equality could gain real ground. In its election manifesto, the Labour Party had committed to holding a referendum on 'gay marriage rights'.[8] Now in their programme for government Fine Gael and Labour committed to following the promises of their respective manifestos by establishing a Constitutional Convention which would provide a report on a number of constitutional issues within the first twelve months of government. 'Provision for same-sex marriage' was listed as one of the items for 'broader constitutional review' in 'a process to ensure that our Constitution meets the challenges of the 21st century'.[9]

In an indicative move, the Labour leader and Tánaiste, Eamon Gilmore, recommended Katherine Zappone to be appointed to Seanad Éireann. Taoiseach Enda Kenny duly nominated Zappone as a Senator and she served in the 24th Seanad, becoming the first openly lesbian member of the Oireachtas. Two openly gay Labour politicians, John Lyons and Dominic Hannigan, also served in that government. In her position as Senator, Zappone ensured that she used the political powers she was granted to voice the now growing opinion that civil partnerships did not constitute equality for same-sex couples. In July 2011, Zappone proposed an amendment to grant same-sex couples equal rights with married couples in terms of citizenship. The amendment was proposed as part of the Civil Law (Miscellaneous Provisions) Bill put forward by the then Minister for Justice and Equality, Alan Shatter of Fine Gael.

Zappone's proposed amendment would simply ensure that civil partners would be subject to the same laws under the Irish Nationality and Citizenship Act which currently discriminated under the naturalisation process by requiring a non-Irish spouse to live in Ireland for three years before being considered for citizenship whereas a civil partner must be resident for at least five years. Zappone's proposal was supported by Senator Bacik and seconded by Independent Senator Sean D. Barrett. Senator Rónán Mullen, who had objected unreservedly to the Civil Partnership Bill, also supported the amendment. Minister Shatter approved Zappone's proposed amendment. This change in legislation was a positive step towards gaining further equality for same-sex couples.

Senator Zappone took the opportunity to voice concern regarding the Civil Partnership Bill in the Seanad debate, stating that:

> the passage of the Civil Partnership and Certain Rights and Obligations of Cohabitants Act 2010 signalled the Government's intention to provide similar rights, protections and responsibilities for same-sex couples as for married couples and viewed this as a major step towards equality for same-sex couples. It is my view that the establishment of a separate institution for same-sex couples, namely, civil partnership, was not the most effective and efficient way to equalise treatment between same-sex and opposite-sex couples. Nor do I think it was the right thing to do ... there remain a number of differences between civil partnership and civil marriage and some of these differences, it would seem to me, can be eradicated with very little debate. [10]

Indeed, the coalition government set about rectifying some of the differences to which Zappone referred. Just weeks after the Seanad debate on Citizenship, a new Finance Bill was signed into law ensuring that civil partners would enjoy the same tax benefits as married couples. The bill was enacted to amend taxation acts 'in relation to the taxation of civil partners and cohabitants as a consequence of the Civil Partnership and Certain Rights and Obligations of Cohabitants Act 2010 and to provide for connected matters'.[11] This was a significant amendment, bearing in mind it was a case against the Revenue Commissioners that was originally launched by Zappone and Gilligan. The amendment had an immediate effect on same-sex families, treating them the same as married couples for tax purposes, including accounting for children in these families.

On 4 October 2011, Marriage Equality officially launched a vibrant new nationwide campaign which they called *Just Love?* Partly the campaign was launched to ensure that activists did not become complacent after the implementation of civil partnership. The main campaign aim was to educate the public to the fact that although civil partnerships offered some rights similar to marriage, it was simply not enough. Full equality for same-sex couples would only be achieved when such couples could avail of full civil marriage, the ultimate goal of Marriage Equality. The new campaign was ambitious and set about telling personal stories of lesbian and gay couples. Before the official launch the group again put its media skills to sound use, producing a short film called *Rory's Story*. The Dublin production company Fail Safe Films produced the film, which was first uploaded onto social media sites in September. The emotional video 'depicted the experience of a young man who is refused medical information about his non-biological mother who is gravely ill'.[12] As the video concludes a voiceover stresses that 'civil partnership neglects the rights between a child and his or her non-biological parent and the consequences are real'. Viewers are then advised to seek more information by contacting the Marriage Equality website. The powerful message was made all the more poignant because film-makers included Evan Barry, the adult child of a same-sex couple. Barry, with Fail Safe Films, went on to make another video in the run-up to the marriage equality referendum called *Every Vote*, calling on people to make their voices heard at the polls.

The *Just Love?* campaign included tactically placed billboards featuring regular lesbian and gay couples. The content of the billboards was also published in newspapers across the country and disseminated through online sources. At the very heart of the campaign was a detailed report, *Missing Pieces*, which highlighted no less than 169 differences between marriage and civil partnership. The report published the results of a major audit funded by Atlantic Philanthropies and the Urgent Action Fund for Women's Human Rights. The audit examined the legal differences between civil partnerships and civil marriage and was conducted by an impressive team of legal specialists.[13] The initial stage was researched by seventeen law graduates with the guidance of Justine Quinn BL. The second stage sought the support of a legal team who provided advice on the various sections of the report which examined rights in relation to the family home, finance, immigration, legal procedures, and between parent and child. The landmark audit was the first detailed examination comparing the legal differences between civil marriage and partnerships and took over a year of intense research. The findings were produced in a glossy, easily accessible report authored by Paula Fagan.

As if proving the implications of the findings, the launch of the audit coincided with an announcement by the Department of Foreign Affairs that there were no plans to change passport applications to recognise same-sex parents. *Missing Pieces* was generally welcomed across the media and political arena. The *Irish Times* reported that 'the Civil Partnership Act, which came into law at the start of the year, contains glaring omissions governing the rights of children and the protection of the family home', which were highlighted by the research.[14] Speaking at the launch, Fagan outlined why the audit was necessary, saying that 'civil partnership was heralded as equality in all but name for same-sex couples but this report firmly and rightly contradicts these untrue claims'.[15] She continued by stating that 'civil partnership is a welcome first step to protect same-sex couples, but it fails to provide equality, civil partnership dismally overlooks the love which same-sex couples have for one another, and most ashamedly, it neglects the bonds between same-sex parents and their children'.[16] Senator Bacik attended the launch and made a pointed reference to it in Seanad Éireann later that day, highlighting how it 'drew a comprehensive and impressive comparison between the rights and responsibilities of civil partnership compared to those relating to civil marriage and drew the conclusion that the civil partnership regime falls short in 169 respects compared to that of marriage'.[17]

Later that month Senator Zappone and Dr Gilligan applied to the Supreme Court to allow them to amend their grounds for appeal. The couple sought to 'include an appeal that Section 2.2. of the Civil Registration Act 2004 was unconstitutional'.[18] In this way the couple were testing the constitutionality of prohibiting them and other same-sex couples from accessing civil marriage. The Supreme Court denied their request. Yet another disappointment for Zappone and Gilligan; however, they were not disheartened and vowed to continue their legal action. On the advice of Justice Liam McKechnie they decided that they would return to the High Court and file new proceedings.[19]

Despite such a negative response from the Supreme Court, Marriage Equality continued to grow, both in the number of supporters and in public recognition of its cause. On 22 October, Marriage Equality won the award for community organisation of the year at the 2011 GALAS, the annual LGBT awards established by the *Gay Community News* and the National LGBT Federation to recognise the contribution of groups and individuals towards Irish society. The following month many of the country's leading artists donated their art to be auctioned as a fundraising event for Marriage Equality. The next step in the campaign was to prepare for the Constitutional Convention promised by the new coalition government.

While the government were debating the process for establishing the convention, Noel Whelan was initially sceptical, writing in the *Irish Times* that 'the programme for government did not define what it meant by a constitutional convention, did not detail its likely composition and was silent on what would happen to any recommendations'.[20] The proposal for the establishment of the convention was released by the government on 28 February 2012. The forum would include a hundred people. Sixty-six would be citizens randomly selected using the electoral register, chosen to ensure representation across Irish society in terms of age, gender, religion and occupation. Thirty-three members would comprise parliamentarians nominated by their parties and taken from across both Houses of the Oireachtas, and members of the Northern Ireland Assembly would be invited. Finally, an independent Chair would be nominated through a proposed resolution of the Houses of the Oireachtas. It was later agreed by consensus to elect Tom Arnold, then CEO of the charity Concern Worldwide, for that prestigious and demanding role.

Initially it was not clear what part interest groups could play in the process; however, this was clarified in a government response to opposition party questions. In June, the government released a statement including the provision that 'interest groups would be able to interact with the convention, including by making submissions, and that the chair and members would be anxious to hear from a representative spectrum of opinion in carrying out their work'.[21] It was also ascertained at this stage that the government would respond to any recommendation made by the convention within four months and that this would happen through debate in the Oireachtas, thus ensuring public awareness of recommendations. In the event that a recommendation for constitutional change was made, the government would ensure a timeframe for a referendum on the issue was included in the public response.[22]

The Constitutional Convention was hailed by political analysts as 'a major experiment in deliberative democracy in Ireland'.[23] The first formal meeting took place on 1 December 2012, at St Patrick's Hall in

Dublin Castle. This first meeting mainly comprised informative sessions for attendees on the history and place of the Irish Constitution as well as the purpose and experience of similar conventions in other countries. A range of politicians, across party divides, were invited to address the first meeting, including the Taoiseach, the Tánaiste and leaders of main parties; Micheál Martin for Fianna Fáil; Gerry Adams for Sinn Féin and Maureen O'Sullivan, an Independent TD.[24] The Constitutional Convention began a rigorous timetable from the first working meeting in January 2013 involving ten weekend-long meetings that continued until 2014. The breakdown of the weekend structure is best described by Healy, Sheehan and Whelan, who were closely following the process in anticipation of the 'same-sex marriage' focus:

> On Saturday mornings an expert panel gave delegates an overview of the legal and constitutional context of whatever issue was being discussed. Then representatives from each side made their case to the whole Convention in plenary session before delegates deliberated in small groups at their tables. Later, each table group reported back to a plenary session and then a question and answer period was held with a panel of stakeholders. On Sunday morning the delegates, having reflected on the issue overnight, debated the wording of the precise recommendation to government on which they would vote. Then they voted on the proposal and the result of the vote was announced.[25]

The convention was established to ensure greater participation from citizens in the democratic process and as such all its activities were open for public scrutiny. A website was established to ensure that the public were notified about upcoming meetings and offered an opportunity to make submissions. The site also published all related documents, deliberations and the names of convention members. The plenary debates were streamed live from this site and the public was actively encouraged to engage with the process. The Chair of the convention, Tom Arnold, would later describe this process as representing 'a significant innovation: this is the first time anywhere in the world randomly selected citizens have worked side by side with elected representatives to propose constitutional change'.[26]

The convention was tasked with examining a number of key areas for constitutional review, including the presidential term of office, voting age and the position of women in the home. The provision of extending marriage to same-sex couples was tabled for examination on the weekend of 13/14 April 2013. Following the established format, representatives from either side of this campaign were invited to address the delegates in a thirty-minute presentation. GLEN, Marriage Equality and the Irish Council for Civil Liberties (ICCL) were invited to present their argument in support of civil marriage for same-sex couples. The opposing view would be presented by the Knights of St Colombanus, the Evangelical Association of Ireland and the Irish Catholic Bishops' Conference. The call for submissions from interested parties was posted and 1,077 submissions were received from the public by the deadline date of 19 March. This was the highest number of submissions received on any one topic during the life of the convention.[27] The submissions were received mainly from individuals and religious institutions but also included those from various interested organisations, including Trinity College Dublin's LGBT union, Amnesty International Ireland, and Family and Life (described as a pro-life organisation).

Tom Arnold examined the submissions in order to draw out the main arguments for and against extending civil marriage, so that delegates could consider all sides of the debate. The arguments in favour of marriage equality were broadly divided into two main sections: equality/discrimination and children's welfare and best interests. Arguments in favour also cited the view that civil partnership was not equality and that the majority of Irish citizens would be supportive of a change in this regard. Arguments against were mainly based on the belief that marriage between a same-sex couple would 'fundamentally redefine marriage' and undermine the Irish Constitution. The 'natural law argument' was also prevalent, as was the belief that 'same-sex marriage is not in the best interests of children'.[28]

Legal and academic experts were invited to present on the core issues, taking public submissions into account. Senior counsel Gerard Durcan addressed the current legal protection of the family and of the institution of marriage by the Irish Constitution. Barrister Dr Sarah Fennell followed on from this topic by outlining how the Constitution could be amended to extend the protection to same-sex couples. She further examined what legislative changes would be required for such an amendment. Barrister Dr Eimear Brown provided context for the first two presentations by offering an overview of protection afforded to same-sex couples and their children in other countries. The final expert presentation was made by Professor Jim Sheehan, a mental health practitioner who addressed the central issue relating to the children of same-sex couples. After a question and answer session delegates convened to their roundtable discussions to consider the information with which they had been provided.

After a lunchbreak it was time for the advocacy group presentations. The first group to present was in support of the extension of marriage to same-sex couples. The speakers were Tiernan Brady, Muriel Walls, Stephen O'Hare, Moninne Griffith, Gráinne Healy, Conor Prendergast and Clare O'Connell. The three main organisations – GLEN, Marriage Equality and ICCL – agreed to make a joint submission due to their common goal and the time limitation of thirty minutes. The speakers included the main drivers of the organisations, while Prendergast and O'Connell as adult children of same-sex couples established a personal record for delegates. Healy, Sheehan and Whelan describe how these two presentations changed the tone: 'they made real the issue that the convention was to discuss that weekend. This was no longer an academic, theoretical or legal discussion.'[29] At the conclusion of their presentation the speakers asked that delegates would advise the government to extend civil marriage to same-sex couples.

Immediately following this session, representatives from advocacy groups opposing marriage for same-sex couples presented. Bishop Leo O'Reilly and Mrs Breda McDonald spoke on behalf of the Irish Catholic Bishops' Conference. Sean Mullan represented the views of the Evangelical Alliance Ireland and Colm Hagen those of the Order of the Knights of St Columbanus. The entire proceedings were watched by the public through live streaming, and LGBT communities around the country organised screenings in key locations such as Rory O'Neill's bar, Pantibar, in Dublin.

Once both groups had presented, delegates convened to their smaller roundtable discussions before the floor was opened to hear discussions from other tables. This generated a heated debate before being presented with a final panel discussion session. The panellists included Colm O'Gorman from Amnesty International Ireland; Dr Conor O'Mahony, a lecturer in constitutional law at University College Cork (UCC); David Quinn, Director of the Iona Institute; Michael Dwyer of Preserve Marriage; and Carol Coulter, former legal editor of the *Irish Times*. While tension was already high in the room, the discussion was again heated and emotional for many. The Sunday morning session, ahead of the voting by delegates, saw emotional contributions by two political representatives of the convention. John Lyons and Jerry Buttimer, both elected TDs, were also gay men. Their sexuality would not normally be of consequence in political matters; now they spoke personally on this topic. Lyons drove right to the centre of the issue, saying that 'anything less than full civil marriage for every single individual is discrimination. Call it anything else, but it is discrimination. And if you're happy to discriminate against people that is your prerogative, but I'm not happy to discriminate against anyone in this Republic and I ask you to remember that today.'[30] Buttimer, who had recently been inspired to come out publicly as a gay man, spoke with true emotion.[31] He told fellow delegates that 'it is because I saw my parents' marriage that I value and cherish marriage. I want to marry the person I love to enhance and enrich my life. Love between two people should never be undermined.'[32]

The result of the convention vote was a remarkable victory for the advocates of marriage equality. Members decided to confine the ballot paper to straightforward questions relating to the issue they were tasked with examining: the provision for same-sex marriage. The main question on the ballot paper asked delegates to vote on the question: 'Should the Constitution be changed to allow for civil marriage for same sex couples?' The answer was overwhelmingly yes. Seventy-nine out of ninety-nine delegates with a voting entitlement voted in favour. Only nineteen delegates voted against, with one delegate recording a no opinion stance. In relation to children, an issue that had remained contentious in the discussions over the weekend, eighty-one delegates voted in favour of the question: 'In the event of changed arrangements in relation to marriage, the State shall enact laws incorporating necessary changed arrangements in regard to the parentage, guardianship and upbringing of children.' Only twelve delegates voted no to this question.[33] In his conclusion to the convention recommendations, Arnold added a note:

> On all the issues balloted, a strong majority emerged.
> Thus, a strong majority favoured amendment of the Constitution to provide for same-sex marriage. A similarly strong majority favoured directive or mandatory wording in the event of such amendment going ahead.

Again a strong majority recommended legislation to accompany any such amendment, to provide specifically for changed arrangements in regard to the parentage, guardianship and upbringing of children. The reason for including this option on the ballot paper was that in the case of same-sex couples in loco parentis to children, at least one parent will not be a genetic parent and therefore the usual rules regarding custody, guardianship etc. would need to be reviewed and – according to the Convention's preference – adapted for this situation.[34]

## Notes

1   Fianna Fáil, *Real Plan, Better Future*, Fianna Fáil Manifesto (2011), p. 31.

2   Fine Gael, *Fine Gael Manifesto* (2011), p. 52.

3   Sinn Féin, *There is a Better Way*, Sinn Féin General Election Manifesto (2011), p. 33.

4   Labour Party, *One Ireland: Jobs, reform, fairness*, Labour Party Manifesto (2011), p. 46.

5   Green Party, *Playing to Our Strengths*, Green Party Manifesto (2011), p. 33.

6   Diarmaid Ferriter, 'Recapturing relevance a huge challenge for FF', *Irish Times* (1 March 2011).

7   Department of the Taoiseach, *Programme for Government 2011* (7 June 2011), p. 2.

8   Labour Party, *One Ireland*, p. 5.

9   Department of the Taoiseach, *Programme for Government*, p. 17.

10  Senator Zappone, 'Civil Law (Miscellaneous Provisions) Bill 2011: Report stage', *Seanad Éireann Debate*, Vol. 209, No. 5 (7 July 2011).

11  Finance (No. 3) Act 2011.

12  Healy, Sheehan and Whelan, *Ireland Says Yes*, p. 113.

13  Inge Clissmann SC, on family home provisions; Kevin Darcy BL and Trevor Redmond BL, parent and child legal provisions; Dearbhla Cunningham BL, Marguerite Bolger SC and Justine Quinn BL, finance provisions; Patrick Dillon Malone BL, immigration provisions; Dr Fiona de Londras, legal procedures provisions; Natalie McDonnell BL, miscellaneous provisions; Catherine Cosgrove BL, Noleen Blackwell, Professor Gerry White, Eilis Barry BL, Camille Loftus and Ciara Murray, additional advice on findings. Paula Fagan, *Missing Pieces: A comparison of the rights and responsibilities gained from civil partnership compared to the rights and responsibilities gained through civil marriage in Ireland*, Dublin, 2011, p. 2.

14  Aoife Carr, 'Group calls for equal marriage rights', *Irish Times* (4 October 2011).

15 'New report reveals 169 differences between civil marriage and civil partnership', press release, Marriage Equality (4 October 2011).
16 Ibid.
17 Senator Ivana Bacik, *Seanad Debates*, Vol. 210, No. 9 (4 October 2011), p. 490.
18 Gavin Reilly, 'Gilligan and Zappone vow to continue with Supreme Court appeal', *The Journal* (23 October 2011).
19 Katherine Zappone, *Submission to the Constitutional Convention on Marriage for Same-Sex Couples* (11 March 2013).
20 Noel Whelan, 'Constitutional convention will have its remit severely pruned', *Irish Times* (25 February 2012).
21 'Government response to opposition views on the proposal to establish a Constitutional Convention', Government of the 31st Dáil (26 June 2012).
22 Ibid.
23 Johan A. Elkink et al., 'Understanding the 2015 Marriage Referendum in Ireland: Context, campaign, and conservative Ireland', *Irish Political Studies*, 32:3 (2017), 361–81, at 2.
24 'Agenda for the inaugural meeting of the convention on the constitution in Dublin Castle' (1 December 2012).
25 Healy, Sheehan and Whelan, *Ireland Says Yes*, p. 4.
26 Tom Arnold, 'Inside the convention on the constitution', *Irish Times* (1 April 2014).
27 Healy, Sheehan and Whelan, *Ireland Says Yes*, p. 4.
28 Convention on the Constitution, *Third Report of the Convention on the Constitution: Amending the Constitution to provide for same-sex marriage* (June 2013), available at: www.constitution.ie (accessed 24 July 2017).
29 Healy, Sheehan and Whelan, *Ireland Says Yes*, p. 1.
30 Ibid., p. 12.
31 Independent.ie reporter, 'Cork Fine Gael deputy Jerry Buttimer comes out saying: I'm a TD who just happens to be gay', *Irish Independent* (30 April 2012), available at: www.independent.ie/irish-news/cork-fine-gael-deputy-jerry-buttimer-comes-out-saying-im-a-td-who-just-happens-to-be-gay-26848351.html (accessed 11 July 2018).
32 Healy, Sheehan and Whelan, *Ireland Says Yes*, p. 12.
33 Convention on the Constitution, *Third Report*.
34 Ibid.

# 7

# Preparing for a revolution

The 1937 Irish Constitution 'reflected the aspirations for our country as they were in the 1930s which was a time when one church had a special place when women were second class citizens and homosexuality was a criminal offence, a time when Europe was at the brink of a second war of a generation'.[1] These words formed the key focus of Tánaiste Eamon Gilmore's address to delegates at the inaugural meeting of the Constitutional Convention. The convention was established to ensure 'participative democracy' in considering changes to the Constitution. In April 2013, delegates at the convention had overwhelmingly called for a constitutional change to extend civil marriage to same-sex couples and, significantly, to include amendments for parental rights in this regard. This outcome was seen as a reflection of public opinion across Ireland. After the results were made public, Gilmore expressed his satisfaction, reiterating that 'our laws reflect the past, not the future'.[2] On this issue in particular, Gilmore continued that 'it's not the role of the State to pass judgement on who a person falls in love with, or who they want to spend their life with'.[3]

The significance of the outcome was recognised by those opposing marriage for same-sex couples. The process had been hailed as a democratic success which engaged rigorous methods for consideration on focus issues. However, Senator Rónán Mullen queried this, asserting that 'some citizen members of the convention felt that they had been pressured by politician members at the tables to support a particular line'.[4] Mullen did not provide evidence to support his assertion that citizen members were pressurised to vote a particular way or prove exactly how the process was, as he maintained, 'flawed'.

Meanwhile a spokesman for the Catholic Communications Office told the *Irish Times* that 'while the result of the constitutional convention is disappointing, only the people of Ireland can amend the constitution. The Catholic church will continue to promote and seek protection for the uniqueness of marriage between a woman and a man, the nature of which best serves children and our society.'[5] This signalled a clear intention from many Catholic advocacy groups to launch a more focused campaign in opposition, should a referendum be called on the issue. The convention recommendations were sent directly to the government, which had committed to hold a debate in the Oireachtas before setting out its response within a four-month timeframe.

The three main organisations supporting marriage equality were naturally exhilarated by the outcome of the convention. GLEN, the ICCL and Marriage Equality had successfully combined their efforts to deliver an informative and persuasive presentation to delegates. The groups recognised that this was only the first step of what would become an intense campaign. The next step was to ensure that the government followed recommendations and set a date for a referendum. It seemed logical for the three groups to continue working together in this regard. GLEN had been involved from the onset in moves to establish civil partnerships in order to ultimately achieve full civil marriage for same-sex couples. Marriage Equality was by now a well-established force working towards this single goal. The ICCL shared this objective; as early as 2006 the group had published *Equality for All Families*, a report 'which concluded that same-sex couples should no longer be barred from entering civil marriage'.[6]

Healy, as Chair of Marriage Equality, called a meeting inviting Brian Sheehan, Director of GLEN, and Mark Kelly, a human rights lawyer and Director of the ICCL, to discuss the way forward. This initial meeting established a continued close working relationship between the groups, which began to meet fortnightly and later weekly to work on campaign tactics. The formal report of the convention was submitted to the Oireachtas for consideration on 2 July; this meant that the government must respond by 2 November, to meet the four-month deadline. In October, Gilmore announced that a referendum would be called before Spring 2015. Just past the deadline, on 5 November, the government formally announced that after considering the recommendations of the convention, a referendum on extending civil marriage to same-sex couples would be held in 2015. The Taoiseach would later address a press conference assuring the public that the government would strongly support a Yes vote for marriage equality.

On 17 December, Alan Shatter addressed the Dáil in his position as Minister for Justice to inform the House that the government had agreed to hold a referendum on marriage for same-sex couples which would take place before mid-2015. Shatter continued by noting his support for a change in the Irish Constitution in this regard and reminded members that banning certain people from marrying should be particularly poignant for Irish people. He described how 'the restrictions on marriage introduced under the Penal Laws were deeply felt. They prevented intermarriage between Catholics and Anglicans and ensured that marriages conducted by Presbyterian ministers were not legally recognised. Those restrictions, which would have seemed reasonable at the time to those who put them in place, were, in more enlightened times, dismantled as deeply unfair and discriminatory.'[7] There followed a ninety-minute debate in the Dáil but rather than debate the issue, all TDs who spoke praised the work of the convention and supported not only a referendum but also wholeheartedly declared their support of extending civil marriage to same-sex couples. TDs across all party divides and Independents alike supported marriage equality. Yvonne Murphy described how with

> all major political parties advocating for a 'Yes' vote, only a handful of national politicians actively campaigned for the 'No' side. They included Independent TD Mattie McGrath, who was the only TD to have indicated an intention to vote against the Referendum at the time the Bill was progressing through the Oireachtas and Independent Senator Rónán Mullen who tabled a number of amendments to the Bill in an effort to provide, inter alia, an avenue for conscientious objection to providing services for same-sex marriages.[8]

On the same day of the formal announcement of the referendum, the Department of Justice and Equality published a briefing note on the Family Relationships and Children Bill 2013; the bill aimed 'to create a legal structure to underpin diverse parenting situations and provide legal clarity on parental rights and duties in diverse family forms'.[9] In the document Minister Shatter noted that the current law on provision of childcare was 'substantially outdated', especially bearing in mind that the Civil Partnership Bill 'did not address the legal status of children in such relationships'.[10] The Law Reform Commission had earlier pointed to the fact that the Civil Partnership Bill 'does not address the relationship between same-sex couples and their children'.[11] The 'diverse family forms' covered by the proposed bill would include 'married families, families that rely on the care of children by members of the extended family, families based on cohabiting couples and [significantly for same-sex couples] civil partnerships'.[12] Additionally, the bill sought to address children born through assisted human reproduction and surrogacy. Within weeks, Shatter published the heads of bill; this was a legislative change that he had personally worked on introducing.

The Children and Family Relationships Bill went to the Joint Oireachtas Committee for Justice for pre-legislative hearings. In its submission to the committee, GLEN described the proposed bill as 'perhaps the greatest family law reform in a generation [which] will be of enormous benefit to the very many children and families, in particular to the very significant numbers of children who are born or being brought up outside the traditional marital family'.[13] Such a ground-breaking legislative proposal inevitably brought with it vocal opposition. The proposed bill inspired Professor Ray Kinsella to establish a group, Mothers and Fathers Matter (MFM). Just as the same key figures arise throughout LGBT rights campaigns in Ireland, the same figures emerge in the campaign opposing marriage equality. The advisory Board of MFM comprised a panel of mainly academics and included David Quinn of the Iona Institute and Dr Thomas Finnegan, former parliamentary advisor to Senator Rónán Mullen. The group described its primary aim as opposing the Children and Family Relationships Bill on the grounds that it is 'unjust because it says mothers and fathers don't matter to children'.[14]

The introduction of the bill would ultimately be put on hold due partly to a series of controversies affecting the Department of Justice and Equality at the start of 2014 which caused Minister Shatter to resign from his position in May of that year. The referendum now dominated the marriage equality campaign and it was a forefront concern for campaigners in opposition. MFM turned its attention to this, announcing that it favoured 'retaining the present definition of marriage because this is in the best interests of children'.[15]

The opposition campaign would reach a controversial high when on 11 January 2014, Rory O'Neill, aka Panti Bliss, appeared on RTÉ's *The Saturday Night Show* with presenter Brendan O'Connor. During the interview O'Connor asked O'Neill what life was currently like for lesbian and gay people living in Ireland. In his response O'Neill noted that because Ireland is a small country most people are related to or know a gay person and therefore they are not prejudiced against LGBT people. He went on to say that 'the only place that you see it's okay to be really horrible and mean about gays is you know on the internet in the comments and you know people who make a living writing opinion pieces for newspapers'.[16] O'Connor followed this up by asking O'Neill to be specific when he questioned him: 'Who are they?' O'Neill replied, 'Oh well the obvious ones. You know Breda O'Brien today, oh my God you know banging on about gay priests and all. The usual suspects, the John Waters and all of those people, the Iona Institute crowd.'[17] The discussion then proceeded to the complications of defining homophobia. O'Neill clarified that 'homophobia can be very subtle … it's like the way you know racism is very subtle. I would say that every single person in the world is racist to some extent because that's how we order the world in our minds. We group people.'[18]

Both journalists Waters and O'Brien, along with David Quinn on behalf of the Iona Institute, contacted RTÉ to make a complaint. This was the beginning of a great controversy, popularly referred to as Pantigate, which placed the issue of marriage equality centre stage in an open debate about homophobia. Days after the interview aired the entire programme was removed from the station's web player. The programme was later uploaded again, with O'Neill's discussion of homophobia and references to individuals and the Iona Institute edited out. RTÉ clarified to *The Journal* that 'last weekend's *The Saturday Night Show* was removed from the Player due to potential issues and for reasons of sensitivity following the death of Tom O'Gorman as would be standard practice in such situations'.[19] In an article posted on *Catholic Ireland*, Susan Gately confirmed that the O'Neill interview aired the same night that Tom O'Gorman, a 'researcher with Iona, was killed in his Dublin home'.[20] Although O'Gorman worked for the Iona Institute, O'Neill had not mentioned him in his interview.

On *The Saturday Night Show* the following week, Brendan O'Connor issued an apology on air. O'Connor noted:

> On *The Saturday Night Show* two weeks ago comments were made by a guest suggesting the journalist and broadcaster John Waters, Breda O'Brien and some members of the Iona Institute are homophobic. These are not the views of RTÉ and we would like to apologise for any upset or distress caused to the individuals named or identified. It is an important part of democratic debate that people must be able to hold dissenting views on controversial issues.[21]

The apology caused distress to Rory O'Neill and to many viewers. Hundreds of complaints were received by RTÉ for issuing such an apology. O'Neill tweeted that he was confused by the apology, questioning 'am I the one with dissenting views on the Iona et al …?'[22] Days later it emerged that RTÉ had not only issued a public apology but the broadcast body had also financially compensated those named by O'Neill in the interview. The Director General of RTÉ, Glen Killane, maintained that after seeking legal advice it was thought wise to offer financial compensation to the tune of €85,000 to Mr Waters, Ms O'Brien and the Iona Institute.[23] In a letter to RTÉ staff, the Director explained that 'having regard for broadcasting compliance issues, the seriousness of the legal complaints, and the decision by the complainants not to accept RTÉ's proposed remedies, we decided that a settlement was the most prudent course of action. Senior counsel was consulted and confirmed that the legal position was far from clear.'[24] The fact that RTÉ is a State-funded broadcaster, earning much of its revenue from licence fees, meant that Killane was publicly answerable for such decision making.

Breda O'Brien described her reaction to O'Neill's comments and the broadcast, noting that 'RTÉ had breached basic rules of fairness and justice by encouraging Rory O'Neill to identify specific people as homophobic who were not there to defend themselves'.[25] Therefore, O'Brien and the others mentioned sought 'a simple clarification and apology'.[26] O'Brien claimed that when RTÉ refused to issue an apology she along with the Iona Institute and John Waters informed the broadcaster that they 'would be forced to defend our good names through the courts if necessary'.[27] What began as a straightforward television interview generated controversy at a national level.

On 30 January, Senator Averil Power brought the issue into Seanad Éireann. Power demanded that the Minister for Communications, Energy and Natural Resources, Labour Minister Pat Rabbitte, be brought in front of the Seanad to discuss why RTÉ had paid compensation to the Iona Institute and to the two named journalists. Power questioned whether the broadcaster had considered other avenues, such as a right to reply or defending the right of an interviewee to express an opinion, before offering financial compensation. In a damning assertion Power stressed that the national broadcaster has a 'responsibility to ensure all voices are heard, not just those with the deepest pockets'.[28] When asked by the leader of the House if the Senator were seeking a debate on the issue, Power was scathing in her assessment of RTÉ's actions and of the Iona Institute's objectives, noting that:

> The motivation of the Iona Institute in bringing the case is clear. It is afraid of the referendum and the fact that at the constitutional convention, in which people heard both sides of the debate over the course of two days, 80% of those involved voted in favour of equality. They voted to put behind the prejudices and discrimination of the past and to ensure all Irish citizens would be treated equally. This is what the Iona Institute is afraid of because it cannot win that debate. It cannot win a fair and open debate, but it has money and influence which it is trying to exercise in this case. RTÉ has a responsibility to ensure no organisation can dictate the terms just because it is influential or has powerful backers.[29]

Power identified how the issue of broadcasting would become central to the referendum campaign.

In an attempt to redress the controversy and show it was capable of open and balanced debate, *The Saturday Night Show* held a discussion on homophobia in its 1 February broadcast. The panel members included Senator Power, Colm O'Gorman and Noel Whelan. Breda O'Brien, John Waters and David Quinn were invited to participate but declined. Susan Philips, an ex-councillor and outspoken commentator, was the only panel member who agreed to represent an opposition to marriage equality. However, a number of other interested parties were invited to be part of the audience and input their comments, including Breda O'Brien's son, the journalist Ben Conroy.

On the same night that the programme was being aired live, O'Neill, in his stage drag persona as Panti Bliss, took to the stage of the National Theatre, the Abbey, to give his Noble Call. The Abbey had established the Noble Call to follow every performance of *The Risen People*, an adaptation of a play by James Plunket set around the Dublin Lockout of 1913. The play ran from 28 November 2013 to 1 February 2014 to commemorate the centenary of the Lockout. The Director of the Abbey, Fiach Mac Conghail, modified the old Irish tradition of storytelling to include a Noble Call, with a range of people invited to address the audience on their chosen topic. Those invited included historians, artists, actors and journalists. Mac Conghail invited O'Neill to give the final Noble Call. The footage of Panti's speech on homophobia would reach a global audience within days and propel the debate on the forthcoming marriage equality referendum to an international forum. The full speech provides an honest and personal view of homophobia as experienced by O'Neill and how the national broadcaster's apology and financial settlement ultimately protected people from being labelled as homophobic rather than question opinions based on oppressive views:

> Hello. My name is Panti and for the benefit of the visually impaired or the incredibly naïve, I am a drag queen, a performer, and an accidental and occasional gay rights activist.
>
> And as you may have already gathered, I am also painfully middle-class. My father was a country vet, I went to a nice school, and afterwards to that most middle-class of institutions – art college. And although this may surprise some of you, I have always managed to find gainful employment in my chosen field – gender discombobulation.
>
> So the grinding, abject poverty so powerfully displayed in tonight's performance is something I can thankfully say I have no experience of.
>
> But oppression is something I can relate to. Oh, I'm not comparing my experience to Dublin workers of 1913, but I do know what it feels like to be put in your place.
>
> Have you ever been standing at a pedestrian crossing when a car drives by and in it are a bunch of lads, and they lean out the window and they shout 'Fag!' and throw a milk carton at you?
>
> Now it doesn't really hurt. It's just a wet carton and anyway they're right – I am a fag. But it feels oppressive.
>
> When it really does hurt, is afterwards. Afterwards I wonder and worry and obsess over what was it about me, what was it they saw in me? What was it that gave me away? And I hate myself for wondering that. It feels oppressive and the next time I'm at a pedestrian crossing I check myself to see what is it about me that 'gives the gay away' and I check myself to make sure I'm not doing it this time.
>
> Have any of you ever come home in the evening and turned on the television and there is a panel of people – nice people, respectable

people, smart people, the kind of people who make good neighbourly neighbours and write for newspapers. And they are having a reasoned debate about you. About what kind of a person you are, about whether you are capable of being a good parent, about whether you want to destroy marriage, about whether you are safe around children, about whether God herself thinks you are an abomination, about whether in fact you are 'intrinsically disordered'. And even the nice TV presenter lady who you feel like you know thinks it's perfectly ok that they are all having this reasonable debate about who you are and what rights you 'deserve'.

And that feels oppressive.

Have you ever been on a crowded train with your gay friend and a small part of you is cringing because he is being SO gay and you find yourself trying to compensate by butching up or nudging the conversation onto 'straighter' territory? This is you who have spent 35 years trying to be the best gay possible and yet still a small part of you is embarrassed by his gayness.

And I hate myself for that. And that feels oppressive. And when I'm standing at the pedestrian lights I am checking myself.

Have you ever gone into your favourite neighbourhood café with the paper that you buy every day, and you open it up and inside is a 500-word opinion written by a nice middle-class woman, the kind of woman who probably gives to charity, the kind of woman that you would be happy to leave your children with. And she is arguing so reasonably about whether you should be treated less than everybody else, arguing that you should be given fewer rights than everybody else. And when the woman at the next table gets up and excuses herself to squeeze by you with a smile you wonder, 'Does she think that about me too?'

And that feels oppressive. And you go outside and you stand at the pedestrian crossing and you check yourself and I hate myself for that.

Have you ever turned on the computer and seen videos of people just like you in far away countries, and countries not far away at all, being beaten and imprisoned and tortured and murdered because they are just like you?

And that feels oppressive.

Three weeks ago I was on the television and I said that I believed that people who actively campaign for gay people to be treated less or differently are, in my gay opinion, homophobic. Some people, people who actively campaign for gay people to be treated less under the law took great exception at this characterisation and threatened legal action against me and RTÉ. RTÉ, in its wisdom, decided incredibly quickly to hand over a huge sum of money to make it go away. I haven't been so lucky.

And for the last three weeks I have been lectured by heterosexual people about what homophobia is and who should be allowed identify it.

Straight people – ministers, senators, lawyers, journalists – have lined up to tell me what homophobia is and what I am allowed to feel oppressed by. People who have never experienced homophobia in their lives, people who have never checked themselves at a pedestrian crossing, have told me that unless I am being thrown in prison or herded onto a cattle train, then it is not homophobia.

And that feels oppressive.

So now Irish gay people find ourselves in a ludicrous situation where not only are we not allowed to say publicly what we feel oppressed by, we are not even allowed to think it because our definition has been disallowed by our betters.

And for the last three weeks I have been denounced from the floor of parliament to newspaper columns to the seething morass of inter-net commentary for 'hate speech' because I dared to use the word 'homophobia'. And a jumped-up queer like me should know that the word 'homophobia' is no longer available to gay people. Which is a spectacular and neat Orwellian trick because now it turns out that gay people are not the victims of homophobia – homophobes are.

But I want to say that it is not true. I don't hate you.

I do, it is true, believe that almost all of you are probably homophobes. But I'm a homophobe. It would be incredible if we weren't. To grow up in a society that is overwhelmingly homophobic and to escape unscathed would be miraculous. So I don't hate you because you are homophobic. I actually admire you. I admire you because most of you are only a bit homophobic. Which all things considered is pretty good going.

But I do sometimes hate myself. I hate myself because I fucking check myself while standing at pedestrian crossings. And sometimes I hate you for doing that to me.

But not right now. Right now, I like you all very much for giving me a few moments of your time. And I thank you for it.[30]

The audience in the Abbey Theatre that evening reacted with positive and approving applause; many gave Panti Bliss a standing ovation. The full speech was uploaded on to YouTube on 2 February and within two days had amassed over 200,000 views. Within a week the video had gone viral, with celebrities including Madonna, Stephen Fry, RuPaul and Graham Norton sharing links to the speech on social media, ensuring the message went international. As of May 2019, over 900,000 views have been logged on YouTube.

The speech generated a large following and T-shirts emblazoned with 'I'm on Team Panti' were sold across the country; all proceeds went to BeLong To Youth Services, a group supporting Lesbian, Gay, Bisexual and Trans young people in Ireland. Groups wearing the T-shirts sprang up across the country over the coming months, gaining much media attention and further discussion about homophobia. For example, on 11 February 2014 a large group infiltrated the audience of the *Prime Time* current affairs programme on RTÉ television and could be seen sitting in the background with their T-shirt message.[31]

## Notes

1 'Constitutional Convention begins', *Irish Times* (1 December 2012).
2 Ruadhan Mac Cormaic, 'Constitutional convention backs extension of marriage rights to same-sex couples', *Irish Times* (15 April 2013).
3 Ibid.
4 Ibid.
5 Ibid.
6 Healy, Sheehan and Whelan, *Ireland Says Yes*, p. 17.
7 Dáil Éireann, 'Third Report of the Constitutional Convention – Same-Sex Marriage: Statements', *Dáil Éireann Debate*, Vol. 825, No. 1 (17 December 2013).
8 Murphy, 'Marriage equality referendum 2015', 322.
9 Department of Justice and Equality, 'Children and Family Relationships Bill 2013: Briefing note' (5 November 2013), p. 1.
10 Ibid., p. 1.
11 Law Reform Commission, *Legal Aspects of Family Relationships* (LRC 101–2010), para. [3.01].
12 Department of Justice and Equality, 'Children and Family Relationships Bill 2013', p. 1.
13 Brian Sheehan, *GLEN Submission to the Joint Oireachtas Committee on Justice, Defence and Equality on the Heads of the Children and Family Relationships Bill* (February 2014).
14 Mothers and Fathers Matter website, available at: https://mothersand-fathersmatter.org/ (accessed 31 March 2017).
15 Ibid.
16 Transcript of interview-related segment on 'Panti's back on', *Broadsheet* (16 January 2014), available at: www.broadsheet.ie/2014/01/16/wisdom-is-bliss/ (accessed 11 April 2017).

17 Ibid.

18 Ibid.

19 Sinead O'Carroll, 'Part of *The Saturday Night Show* removed from RTÉ Player over "legal issues"', *The Journal* (15 January 2014).

20 Susan Gately, 'RTÉ apologises for "homophobic" accusations on Saturday show', Catholic Ireland.Net (28 January 2014), available at: www.catholicireland.net/rte-apologises-homophobic-accusations-saturday-show/ (accessed 11 April 2017).

21 Aoife Barry, 'RTÉ apologises for "distress" caused by Saturday Night Show guest's comments', *The Journal* (26 January 2014).

22 Mullally, *In the Name of Love*, p. 255.

23 Aishling Phelan, 'Rory O'Neill wants personal apology from RTÉ', *Irish Independent* (10 February 2014).

24 Deputy Stephen S. Donnelly, 'Broadcasting (Amendment) Bill 2014: First stage', *Dáil Éireann Debate*, Vol. 833, No. 2 (5 March 2014).

25 Mullally, *In the Name of Love*, p. 256.

26 Ibid.

27 Ibid.

28 Senator Averil Power, 'Order of business', *Seanad Éireann Debate* (30 January 2014).

29 Ibid.

30 Panti Bliss (Rory O'Neill) 'A Noble Call at the Abbey Theatre', full transcript in Shaun Connolly, 'Buttimer and Panti drown out empty rhetoric in homophobia debate', *Irish Examiner* (8 February 2014).

31 Brian O'Reilly, 'Team Panti supporters infiltrate Prime Time audience', *Irish Independent* (12 February 2014).

# 8

# Yes Equality

The matter of RTÉ's payment of compensation was brought before the Minister of Communications, Pat Rabbitte, to discuss in Dáil Éireann on 6 February 2014. The Minister was confronted with statements by Deputies John Lyons, Jerry Buttimer, Michael Colreavy, Clare Daly, Luke 'Ming' Flanagan, Catherine Murphy and Mick Wallace. All of the Deputies condemned RTÉ's actions. Lyons noted how RTÉ was responsible for moderating and facilitating 'robust debate on issues of social concern, particularly at this time on issues around LGBT rights and equality. After *The Saturday Night Show* several weeks ago, RTÉ's decision to pay out a reported €85,000 in compensation has severely damaged public confidence in our national broadcaster.'[1] Buttimer concurred, noting how RTÉ 'was erroneous and wrong in what it did in this case … Our public service broadcaster has an obligation to provide balanced, responsible and fair transmission of social matters and issues.'[2] Clare Daly summarised the feelings of the Deputies, noting that:

> Brendan O'Connor in the apology offered said it is an important part of democratic debate that people should be entitled to hold dissenting views on controversial subjects. That means, however, one also has to have the right to express a different opinion on that dissenting view and call it by its proper name. As Deputy Buttimer said, if someone is known to be a racist, has expressed racist views, and we call them a racist, are we to then to [sic] apologise to them for calling them by the right name?[3]

Rabbitte ultimately maintained that 'while RTÉ is answerable as a public body, it does not, and should not, operate under political supervision, either at ministerial or parliamentary level'.[4] The Minister refused to intervene in a decision that had already been made and acted on by RTÉ management.

However, Rabbitte would not avoid the issue easily. Senator Zappone brought forward a private member's motion to the Seanad less than two weeks later, on 18 February. Zappone clarified her objective to identify 'the importance of having a public debate on the issues of free speech, homophobia and the public service role of the State broadcaster in such debates'.[5] This motion was brought forward to ensure clarification of the broadcaster's role in prepara-tion of the forthcoming referendum on marriage equality. Minister Rabbitte was present because, as Zappone noted, 'political leadership can ensure that debate on marriage equality is conducted in a fair, open and impartial manner. Impartial means without prejudice and that raises the bar very high.'[6] Furthermore, the Senator acknowl-edged that 'Rory O'Neill has done a great service to our country and wider global LGBT and other human rights movements when exercising his absolute and unrestricted right to hold opinions with-out interference ... [w]hen he further exercised his human right to freedom of expression ... both on *The Saturday Night Show* and on the stage of the Abbey Theatre'.[7]

Marriage Equality and GLEN were present in the visitors' gallery for the debate when the motion was seconded by Ivana Bacik. Senator Bacik summed up the motion, noting that it moves to recognise 'the importance of having a public debate on free speech, homophobia and the public service role of the State broadcaster and explores the issues in the context of the forthcoming referendum on marriage equality'.[8] The Minister's response was to insist that RTÉ should be left to run the national broadcast service without any political inter-vention, noting that 'we rely on broadcasters to provide a forum for matters of public debate and, indeed, controversy and to ensure that, when these take place, the necessary level playing field is provided for all concerned.'[9]

On 5 March, Independent TD Stephen Donnelly introduced a pri-vate member's bill into Dáil Éireann stemming from what he termed 'the scandal known as Pantigate'.[10] The Broadcasting (Amendment) Bill 2014 proposed to remove all mention of the 'subjective term "offence" from the duties of broadcasters'.[11] Donnelly noted that this change would ensure that the national broadcaster could operate for the benefit of all Irish citizens. He noted that the current 2009 legislation 'asks RTÉ not to broadcast anything that might cause offence but, at the same time, to represent minority views that we do not often hear and that may, for whatever reason, cause some people offence', and therefore the legislation required a change.[12] The proposed legislation was presented as a simple change that would ensure groups or individuals could not claim to be offended by certain broadcasts which were debating issues or representing a minority viewpoint. The bill went to the second stage as a Private Member's Motion on 11 April 2014. In his response Minister Rabbitte voiced a concern that changing the broadcasting legislation in this way may 'turn the national broadcaster or any other broadcaster into a version of *The Jerry Springer Show*'.[13] The motion went to a Dáil vote on 15 April and was defeated 44 votes to 76.[14]

The entire controversy, first stemming from Rory O'Neill's interview on *The Saturday Night Show*, opened a background debate on the forthcoming referendum. However, as Healy, Sheehan and Whelan testified, the apology and compensation awarded by the national broadcaster meant that throughout the campaign 'again and again Yes campaigners were to be charged with labelling those opposed to marriage equality as homophobic, which allowed the key advocates of a No vote to talk of the oppressed, silent No majority who were too afraid to speak out'.[15] The three main groups running the Yes campaign were ever more conscious of organising a focused and professional drive and sought advice from the commercial sector. A sub-group was set up to decide on how to market the Yes campaign; members included those experienced in marketing from across the three member groups: Natalie Weadick and Brian Sheehan (GLEN), Walter Jayawardene (ICCL), and Andrew Hyland and Orla Howard (Marriage Equality).[16]

In August 2014, it was agreed to hire the Dublin-based company Language Communication Ltd to form the brand of the campaign and its partner FUSIO to manage the digital campaign. Adam May, Director of the communications company, had devised what would become the name of the new combined organisation: Yes Equality. The name was genius in its simplicity. The full title; Yes Equality: The Campaign for Civil Marriage Equality, or Tá Comhionannas: Feachtas Do Pósadh Sibhialta, explained the exact aims of the new organisation in terms of equality for all Irish citizens. This was the formal establishment of the one organisation working on securing a Yes majority vote in the referendum on marriage equality. The steering group was set up with Healy, Sheehan and Mark Kelly overseeing the strategy.

Their first plan of action was a 'register to vote' campaign. To ensure individuals were placed on the 2015 Register of Electors, 25 November 2014 was highlighted as the cut-off date. Yes Equality devised a clever tactic of focusing on voter registration through which it could indirectly promote the Yes vote. Ireland, as with many countries, often has a low voter turnout for referendums. The lowest turnout is traditionally among the younger population of under twenty-fives, a group also most likely to support the extension of civil marriage to all. The campaign received the support of organisations across the country, including trade unions and the Union of Students in Ireland. The Trade Union IMPACT had already voted unanimously to support a Yes vote at the forthcoming referendum.

From the onset the Taoiseach, Enda Kenny, gave his full endorsement to the 'register to vote' campaign. This was closely followed by other politicians, including the leaders of all the main political parties. Following a cabinet reshuffle Joan Burton was nominated as Tánaiste and leader of the Labour Party; she supported the register to vote campaign, as did Sinn Féin leader, Gerry Adams and Fianna Fáil leader, Micheál Martin. There were a large number of high-profile celebrity endorsements, including Anjelica Houston, Christy Moore and Dara O' Briain. Colin Farrell wrote an open letter of support to the *Sunday World* newspaper, stating that 'it's time to right the scales of justice here. To sign up and register to vote next year so that each individual's voice can be heard. How often do we get to make history in our lives? Not just personal history. Familial. Social. Communal. Global. The world will be watching. We will lead by example.'[17]

An official launch on 3 November was held in Cork, led by disability rights activist, Joanne O'Riordan and Kilkenny All-Ireland Champion hurler, Eoin Murphy. At the launch O'Riordan stressed that it was 'younger voters in this referendum [who] have the chance to make a real difference. This voter registration campaign is a critical first step in getting the vote out. We cannot afford to miss a single vote and if you're not registered you can't vote for civil marriage equality.'[18] Murphy further highlighted that 'next year we will have an important referendum on civil marriage equality. We want to make sure that no one misses the opportunity to have their voice heard on polling day. We are asking people to join us in registering to vote so that they can be part of creating a fairer Ireland for all.'[19]

The register to vote campaign was an immense success, especially considering the short term over which it ran, only three weeks. By 25 November deadline thousands of students had registered to vote on their respective campuses; in UCC over 3,700 people registered, in Trinity College Dublin over 3,000 people; in University College Dublin 4,000 people and in NUI Maynooth over 2,500 people registered.[20] These figures provide just a small example of the thousands of people encouraged to register which can be accredited specifically to the upcoming referendum on marriage equality. The numbers of students who registered on the UCC campus accounted for 20 per cent of the entire student body. That student campaign was led by the auditor of the UCC LGBT society, James Upton.[21] These results alone were a success, and when the option to be added on a supplementary register was later opened before the referendum date an even greater upsurge of registrations would be seen.

In June 2015, Fine Gael used the register to vote campaign as an example of how electoral procedure should be changed in Ireland. In its submission to the electoral commission, Fine Gael wrote, 'the extensive registration drives undertaken by the Yes Equality campaigns and the Union of Students in Ireland for the referendum on marriage equality in 2015 showed the importance of ensuring maximum registration. We believe the Electoral Commission should communicate directly with schools to ensure students understand the registration process.'[22]

However, the campaign's success went far beyond these impressive figures. The vote to register campaign mobilised huge numbers of people to support the Yes Equality campaign across the country and brought the issue of equality foremost in the minds of young voters. A major part of this success was undoubtedly due to the social media side of the Yes Equality drive. Craig Dwyer had been a staff member of GLEN since 2013. Dwyer worked with Diarmuid MacAonghusa, Director and founder of Fusio web designers and online strategists. Together, Dwyer and Fusio created a 'pledge to vote' Facebook page and app.[23] Dwyer set about establishing what would burgeon into an impressive and vibrant social media drive. The Twitter hashtag #registertovote witnessed 1,900 mentions and a reach to over six million Irish Twitter accounts in just three weeks.[24] Celebrities such as Colin Farrell posted pictures of themselves with a downloaded version of the Yes Equality poster emblazoned with 'I'm ready to vote'.

At the end of the successful register to vote campaign, it was time for Yes Equality to form its main campaign strategy. When staff from the newly formed group met on 8 January 2015 they had no campaign office, no funding and no organised plan. The referendum date had not been announced but the understanding was that it would occur in early May. Marriage Equality had designed a referendum strategy to present to potential funders. Its 'Road Map to a Referendum' included 'key elements that would appear in the campaign, including canvasser mobilisation, media activity, a bus tour and engagement with strategic partners, such as children's organisations'.[25]

The marriage equality debate erupted onto radio and television stations across the country from the onset of 2015. Panel discussions, interviews and debates on issues relating to marriage for same-sex couples were predominant stories across all forms of media. On 18 January, in an interview with presenter Miriam O'Callaghan on RTÉ radio, the Minister for Health, Leo Varadkar, came out as a gay man. This was an unexpected and unprecedented move for a serving cabinet Minister. Varadkar became the first openly gay Irish cabinet Minister and in 2017 would go on to become the first openly gay Taoiseach. He was clear that the upcoming referendum was the reason for this personal disclosure. He admitted that 'what I really want to say is that I'd like the referendum to pass because I'd like to be an equal citizen in my own country, the country in which I happen to be a member of Government, and at the moment I'm not'.[26] Healy, Sheehan and Whelan describe this as 'an extraordinary moment that ignited the debate on the referendum'.[27]

Indeed, the debate was truly ignited. The following evening at the launch night of RTÉ television's weekly panel discussion, *Claire Byrne Live*, the debate raged on the issue of marriage equality. In a satellite feed from Los Angeles, the Dublin-born actor Colin Farrell drove home his support for extending marriage to same-sex couples. The heartfelt plea to Irish voters, in which he described how his brother, Eamon, had left Ireland in order to marry his long-term partner Stephen Mannion, later went viral on social media sites. Both sides of the debate were represented, with the No side being presented by journalist Breda O'Brien. A live feed from Newcastle was aired with Dr Sharon James of the Coalition for Marriage group which had unsuccessfully campaigned against the introduction of marriage for same-sex couples in England. Throughout the debates on this programme the issue of parental rights and the legal situation of children of same-sex couples dominated.

Government Ministers were conscious of ensuring that the referendum would be based on a simple Yes or No answer on extending marriage to same-sex couples. To avoid complicating this issue with questions relating to the children of such relationships, it was imperative to bring Alan Shatter's proposed Children and Family Relationships Bill before the Dáil. The bill was brought forward by the recently appointed Minister for Justice, Frances Fitzgerald, on 17 February 2015. The *Irish Times*, in a rather sensational headline, announced 'Gay adoption law due before same-sex marriage referendum'.[28] In a statement given to the *Irish Examiner*, Minister Fitzgerald clarified that 'some of the debate has done a disservice to the wide range of the bill, in terms of assuming that it's about one aspect only and linking it to the referendum, that's not true … It's a very wide-ranging bill, that has implications for many diverse family types.'[29]

The bill was supported by the main political parties and passed the Dáil on 12 March. It subsequently passed the Seanad on 30 March. During the process of debate Senator Jim Walsh resigned from Fianna Fáil because of his party's support of the bill. The *Irish Independent* reported that 'there had been speculation that the Wexford politician would be stripped of the whip due to him opposing the party's stance on the landmark bill'.[30] The bill was signed into law by President Michael D. Higgins on 6 April 2015 although it would be another year before the changes would be effected. Minister Fitzgerald was indeed correct in her assertion that this bill was wide ranging; it essentially modernised the laws surrounding parenting to include diverse family backgrounds. The 100-page bill included 170 sections taking into account the 'best interests of the child [as] paramount in decisions on custody, guardianship and access'.[31] This law updated many aspects of central concern for same-sex-headed families, including eligibility for adoption and establishing guidelines for assisted reproduction and donor-conceived children.

It was an insightful move to pass this legislation before the referendum on marriage equality. The government and all parties involved did not want the referendum question complicated in any way. By ensuring the parenting legislation was passed first, it was envisaged that the referendum could focus simply on a Yes or No vote to extend marriage to same-sex couples. However, the legislation which promised to protect the families of same-sex couples did not pass into law easily. Over one year after the bill was signed by President Higgins, the concerns of Dr Brian Tobin of NUI Galway were reported in the *Irish Examiner*. Tobin described how 'sections 20 to 23 of the Children and Family Relationships Act 2015 had not been commenced which would allow the child's mother and her same-sex spouse to apply to the court for a declaration the spouse is a parent of the child'.[32] Tobin went on to explain that even at that stage in May 2016, 'only the woman who gave birth to the child is allowed to be registered as its mother on the birth certificate and her spouse, the child's second female parent, is not allowed to be registered as a parent because the law does not yet recognise her as such given the State's failure to commence the relevant provisions of the Children and Family Relationships Act 2015'.[33]

## Notes

1   Dáil Éireann, 'RTÉ Compensation Payment', *Dáil Éireann Debate*, Vol. 829, No. 3 (6 February 2014), p. 103.
2   Ibid., pp. 1–4.
3   Ibid., p. 105.
4   Ibid.
5   Senator Katherine Zappone, 'Free Speech, Homophobia and Public Service Role of State Broadcaster: Motion [Private Members]', *Parliamentary Debates: Seanad Éireann*, Vol. 229, No. 13 (18 February 2014).
6   Ibid.
7   Ibid.
8   Ibid.
9   Ibid.
10  Dáil Éireann, 'Broadcasting (Amendment) Bill 2014: First stage', *Parliamentary Debates: Dáil Éireann*, Vol. 833, No. 2 (5 March 2014).
11  Ibid.
12  Ibid.
13  'Broadcasting (Amendment) Bill 2014: Second stage [Private Members]', *Parliamentary Debates: Dáil Éireann*, Vol. 837, No. 4 (11 April 2014).

14  'Broadcasting (Amendment) Bill 2014: Second stage (resumed)', *Parliamentary Debates: Dáil Éireann*, Vol. 838, No. 1 (15 April 2014).

15  Healy, Sheehan and Whelan, *Ireland Says Yes*, p. 22.

16  Ibid., p. 23.

17  As cited by Joanna Robinson, 'Read Colin Farrell's impassioned, personal plea for marriage equality in Ireland', *Vanity Fair* (16 November 2014).

18  Niall Shanahan, 'YES Equality, voter registration campaign launch', *Impact Member's e-bulletin* (7 November 2014), available at: http://impacttradeunion.newsweaver.com/newsletter/1b0q0v5nqab (accessed 26 April 2017).

19  Ibid.

20  'Yes Equality: Thousands register to vote ahead of marriage referendum next year', *GLEN News* (25 November 2014), available at: www.glen.ie/news-post.aspx?contentid=27777 (accessed 26 April 2017).

21  Catherine Healy, 'Why young voters mobilised for same sex marriage', *Irish Times* (23 May 2015).

22  Fine Gael, 'Submission re Electoral Register' (June 2015), p. 2. Available at: Joint Committee on Environment, Culture and the Gaeltacht: Public Consultation on an electoral commission in Ireland, Houses of Oireachtas (14 January 2016), www.oireachtas.ie/www.oireachtas.ie/parliament/oireachtasbusiness/committees_list/environmentcultureandthegaeltacht/electoralcommission/%20/%22 (accessed 2 June 2018).

23  Healy, Sheehan and Whelan, *Ireland Says Yes*, p. 27.

24  Ibid., p. 28.

25  Ibid., p. 31.

26  Ciaran D'Arcy, 'Leo Varadkar: "I am a gay man," Minister says', *Irish Times* (18 January 2015).

27  Healy, Sheehan and Whelan, *Ireland Says Yes*, p. 34.

28  Stephen Collins, 'Gay adoption law due before same-sex marriage referendum', *Irish Times* (21 January 2015).

29  'Fitzgerald: Family Relationships Bill not linked to gay marriage referendum', *Irish Examiner* (2 March 2015).

30  Niall O'Connor and John Downing, 'Fianna Fáil senator Jim Walsh resigns from party over his opposition to Children and Family Relationship Bill', *Irish Independent* (26 March 2015).

31  Department of Justice and Equality website, available at: www.justice.ie/en/JELR/Pages/WP15000315 (accessed 16 June 2018).

32  Noel Baker, 'Same-sex parents "in legal quagmire"', *Irish Examiner* (19 May 2016).

33  Ibid.

# 9

# The campaign in action

The wording for the proposed Thirty-fourth Amendment to the Irish Constitution was 'clear and precise'.[1] In January 2015, it was agreed at a special cabinet meeting that the referendum would consider introducing a declaration into the Irish Constitution that 'marriage may be contracted in accordance with the law by two persons without distinction as to their sex'.[2] The need for Yes Equality to establish themselves in an office space became all the more urgent. Marie Hamilton from GLEN finally secured an office at Clarendon House in the centre of Dublin. It was a compact space but the location was ideal; Monnine Griffith and Andrew Hyland left their Marriage Equality offices and set up in the Clarendon Street premises along with volunteer Joe Hayes.[3] This would become the vibrant hub of the Yes Equality campaign, with more than thirty people packed into these offices over the coming weeks.

On 21 January, the Thirty-fourth Amendment of the Constitution (Marriage Equality) Bill 2015 was initiated in Dáil Éireann. In accordance with procedure, the following week the Minister for the Environment, Community and Local Government, Alan Kelly, established a Referendum Commission. The main objective of the commission was 'to promote public awareness of the referendum and encourage the electorate to vote at the poll'.[4] Mr Justice Kevin Cross was nominated as Chairperson. The following month Taoiseach Enda Kenny announced that the referendum would take place on 22 May 2015. The vote would happen alongside a further proposed amendment to the Constitution to reduce the eligibility age of presidential candidates from thirty-five to twenty-one.

In March, the Referendum Commission launched its awareness campaign, including an independent guide published in booklet form and distributed to over two million homes in the Irish State. The guide contained a short description of each proposed constitutional amendment. Regarding the question of extending civil marriage to same-sex couples, it explained that 'the Constitution does not define marriage and it does not set out who is entitled to marry or who is not entitled to marry. The rules about who is entitled to marry are set out in legislation. The courts have decided that marriage is a union between a man and a woman. This has been reflected in legislation.'[5] The booklet also clarified what would happen if the referendum vote were passed: 'the Constitution will provide that two people may marry each other whether they are of opposite sex or of the same sex. The courts have decided that a married couple with or without children constitute a "Family" in the Constitutional sense.'[6] The clear reasoning extended to describing exactly how laws would be changed or where they would remain the same if the referendum vote were successful. 'Two people of the same sex will be able to marry each other, just as two people of the opposite sex may marry ... The Constitutional status of marriage will remain unchanged ... A marriage between two people of the same sex will have the same status under the Constitution as a marriage between a man and a woman.'[7]

Once the referendum date was called campaigning became an immense battle on both sides of the question and for many of the campaigners it was deeply personal. The referendum debate seemed to dominate every aspect of Irish society over the coming months. Within days of the announcement, a remarkable scene unfolded in the church of St Nicholas of Myra in Francis Street, at the heart of inner-city Dublin, when Fr Martin Dolan took to the pulpit. Fr Dolan, a Catholic priest, had served fifteen years as the parish priest there. At his Saturday evening mass, Dolan addressed the topic of marriage equality in his sermon and announced that he was in support of the Yes campaign. While this was an unusual move by a Catholic priest, to express what was considered an opinion in contradiction with Catholic ethos, what he did next was even more unexpected. In an unprecedented move, Fr Dolan announced that he was in fact a gay man. In an instant, his congregation reacted to the priest coming out about his sexuality at the pulpit by overwhelmingly supporting him with a standing ovation. The event gained an incredible amount

of media attention, with often sensational but also celebratory headlines across the island of Ireland from such diverse sources as the
*Belfast Telegraph*, *Irish Sun* and *Skibbereen Eagle*.[8] The story managed
to gain attention globally, especially in the UK and USA, with the
*Guardian* announcing 'Dublin priest tells congregation he is gay and
wins standing ovation', and the *Huffington Post* 'gay priest comes out
to parishioners and gets a surprising response'.[9]

A number of Catholic priests openly supported the Yes campaign
and criticised the hierarchy of the Church for their opposition. On
10 March, Fr Iggy O'Donovan wrote to the *Irish Times* calling for a
Yes vote in the referendum.[10] O'Donovan was critical of the stance
taken by Catholic bishops, fundamentalists and members of the Iona
Institute for views that he maintained would be damaging to the
Catholic Church in Ireland. The number of Catholic priests who
went against the direction of their bishops reflected a growing awareness from within the Church's ranks that there was a need for reform,
especially in light of greatly reduced attendance at mass over recent
decades. Founder of the left-wing group, the Association of Catholic
Priests, Fr Brendan Hoban, estimated that approximately 25 per cent
of clergy would support and vote Yes at the upcoming referendum.[11]
However, the group refused to 'adopt a position in favour or against
the marriage referendum' and appealed for a 'respectful and civilised
debate'.[12]

Other Catholic priests attempted to override this show of support
for same-sex unions. After O'Donovan's letter appeared in the *Irish
Times*, a Carmelite priest, Fr John Britto, launched into a sermon
at his Saturday evening mass in St Mary's Star of the Sea church
in Annagry, Co. Donegal staunchly advocating against extending
marriage to same-sex couples. Fr Britto criticised Donegal GAA[13]
footballer Éamon McGee for openly supporting the Yes campaign.
He went further, insisting that same-sex unions had been a 'problem'
since the days of Sodom and Gomorrah.[14] Ultimately, Britto insisted
that even 'nature does not approve a same-sex union, [because]
nature does not give them a child'.[15] The priest could not have anticipated the reaction he would receive from his congregation. Some
of those attending the mass walked out of the church in protest and
this reaction was reported, perhaps in an exaggerated manner, in
newspapers across the country. Meanwhile the Church of Ireland
issued a statement declaring that it would not direct its parishioners

to vote either Yes or No in the upcoming referendum: 'The Church of Ireland draws the attention of its members to its own doctrinal position, but does not direct its members how to vote. The Church encourages people to vote according to their conscience.'[16]

National newspapers were awash with similar stories relating to the upcoming referendum when Yes Equality officially launched its referendum campaign in the Pillar Room of the Rotunda Hospital on 9 March 2015. The civil society group was joined in support by representatives from across trade unions, faith-based groups, social justice organisations and other civil society groups. The *Irish Times* reported positively about the 'large attendance at the event'.[17] A number of the attendees were high-profile politicians from across party political divides, including the Tánaiste, Joan Burton; Labour Party Minister, Alex White; Fianna Fáil Senator, Averil Power; and Fine Gael Minister, James Reilly. The event was chaired by journalist Charlie Bird, who later compiled a book including fifty-two personal stories from gay and lesbian people across Ireland about what life was like for them growing up gay in the country.[18] Gráinne Healy summed up the view of Yes Equality and the future pursuit of a Yes vote, stating emphatically at the launch, 'we are the family values campaign … We value love, commitment and family security.'[19] This statement was echoed by Kieran Rose, who also noted how 'Irish people have, with characteristic generosity and fairness, supported emancipation of lesbian and gay people over the past 20 years … we are appealing to the same values again'.[20]

The following day Mark Garrett, a Labour Party official who had been brought in to advise Yes Equality in the run-up to the referendum, wrote a blunt memo to members of the group. In it he stressed, 'the current tone and pace of the campaign is being interpreted by many as taking victory for granted. The campaign does not look or feel like one that is only 73 days or 10 weeks away from its conclusion. All of our experience and the campaign research shows that this is a campaign that should be won but could be very easily lost.'[21] The memo also advised on restructuring, including the final decision to make Healy and Sheehan joint campaign Directors. Meetings of the executive committee were organised for every second day, which would increase to daily within six weeks of the referendum. The memo and the advice shook the Yes Equality team into a more driven and focused campaign.

The more driven focus was led, in part, by Noel Whelan, who had been informally advising the group up to this point. Now Whelan officially joined the campaign. Sheehan describes this as a turning point. Declaring how 'the win wouldn't have happened without him [Whelan]. Our challenge was to develop a strategy that honed both what GLEN and Marriage Equality knew. We came at it very differently. Marriage Equality could reach out to the public and the LGBT community in a way that we couldn't. Noel in effect merged our assets with a clear strategic view about how the referendum should play out. When Noel came in, we had a clear chance of winning the referendum.'[22] Likewise, Ailbhe Smyth attested that 'it would be hard to overestimate Noel's role. He knew how campaigns worked and how Ireland worked. I can't imagine that the campaign would have been as successful without him.'[23]

Also on 10 March, the Executive Director of Amnesty International Ireland, Colm O'Gorman, launched Amnesty's campaign for a Yes vote outside the most politically prominent site in modern Irish history, the General Post Office (GPO).[24] In one line O'Gorman appropriately summarised the views of many in the country: 'love does not discriminate, and neither should our laws'.[25] In the wake of such well-received Yes campaign launches, an Ipsos MRBI poll conducted on behalf of the *Irish Times* showed that 74 per cent of people would vote Yes while the No side was as low as a predicted 26 per cent of the vote.[26]

It was now time to drive a focused campaign across the country but at what financial cost? When Simon Coveney, then Fine Gael Director of the referendum campaign, asked Yes Equality why it was not fundraising there was a realisation that the campaign only had €30,000 in the bank at the start of March. Money for the Yes cause had been donated through various initiatives. Denise Charlton and Paula Fagan had run a successful and vibrant fundraising campaign for Marriage Equality under the hashtag #ShareTheLove. The women drove high-profile fundraising events with the call 'together we can make history'. #ShareTheLove launched in January 2015 with the intention of running until Valentine's Day. However, the initiative was so successful it continued into March, and on the first day of that month a large event was hosted at the Harbour Bar in Bray at which musicians, comedians and DJs entertained donors. Other smaller activities were organised by dedicated supporters through unique events, such as a local Dublin artist, Joy Ní Dhomhnaill, who auctioned a painting at Thomas Reid's pub to make €350. Such instances were tremendously appreciated by the Yes Equality campaign but they needed to step up fundraising in order to meet costs during the final weeks before the referendum. Simon Nugent, an experienced political advisor and a volunteer, estimated that the campaign would need in the region of €300,000.

In early March, Denise Charlton and Karen Ciesielski, Head of External Development for the ICCL, met to organise a targeted fundraising plan. They urged campaign organisers to increase fundraising activities online and through direct outreach as well as organising numerous fundraising events. One of the most vibrant aspects of the Yes Equality campaign was a pop-up shop in St Stephen's Green Shopping Centre in the centre of Dublin. The shop sold merchandise including T-shirts, tote bags, jackets, badges and posters. By the end of the campaign over 6,500 T-shirts, 2,300 tote bags and 800 hi-vis jackets had been sold and an impressive half a million Tá and Yes badges. As Noel Whelan noted, 'this was the campaign that made political wearables trendy in Ireland'.[27] Not only did the merchandise sales help fundraising, but, more importantly, as Ailbhe Smyth testified, 'it [also] gave the campaign tremendous visibility'.[28]

Dedicated volunteers ran social media campaigns and helped oversee two highly successful crowd-funding appeals. The crowd-funding pages were set up by Ciesielski. The first appeal sought a target of €100,000. Over €50,000 was donated by 700 people in a week which allowed the 'Yes Equality Bus Tour' to be launched. Campaigners put out a further call for money to fund the poster campaign. That first crowd-fund broke Yes Equality's expectations by securing €107,040, donated by 1,431 people. The second crowd-funding drive requested €50,000 to fund the production and delivery of one million booklets to be delivered to houses across the country. The call was answered by 858 people and raised a total of €51,520. These two campaigns were a triumph and raised a total of €158,560, much needed money.

With money now coming in, the central focus shifted on to what the campaigners called 'the "million in the middle"—mostly older, undecided voters'.[29] With Whelan based at Clarendon Street offices from 24 March the motivation of the campaign increased. During Whelan's first morning at the office, Tiernan Brady, Policy Director of GLEN, described how during a news report of the Scottish

Independence referendum he spotted a young woman in a background shot with a home-made poster emblazoned with 'I'm Voting Yes, Ask Me Why' written on it.[30] Whelan instantly grasped at this concept. It would become the very heart of their campaign. These words were not just 'a slogan but a strategy'.[31] Once the campaign leaders accepted this tactic, they decided that the way to proceed was to get people out on the street talking to voters, knocking on doors and answering people's questions. Why am I voting Yes? The door-to-door campaign went nationwide. Volunteers signed up in their droves to canvass in their areas and the Yes Equality campaign took on a life of its own. Volunteers included a vast range of people identifying this issue as one of basic equality and not just of LGBT interest. They comprised gay men, lesbians, their mothers and fathers, their friends and supporters, people who believed in equality of human rights.

In order to reach more people and to generate more discussions about 'I'm Voting Yes, Ask Me Why', Moninne Griffith came up with the ingenious idea of the Yes Equality Bus Tour. The tour started on 22 April and continued for four weeks until the referendum. During the twenty-nine-day campaign, the bus toured eighty towns and twenty-six counties, covering eleven thousand kilometres and involving seventy Yes Equality organisations. Kerryann Conway, Managing Director of Conway Communications, worked closely with Vivienne Clarke of the Yes Equality communication team to engage local media in towns and cities before the bus arrived. Fifty volunteers representing a cross-section of society took to the bus and travelled across the country to explain why they would be voting Yes. The route and logistics were carefully planned and activated by Griffith along with Mary McDermott, who became a key organiser.

The bus was launched at Dublin City Hall, and Services Industrial Professional and Technical Union (SIPTU), a trade union representing over 180,000 workers, celebrated this with its own news release describing the crowd who arrived to send the bus off on its tour. 'The well-wishers included mothers, fathers, grandmothers and grandfathers who queued to get on the bus, symbolising the significance of the tour which carries the hope for equality for all their children and grandchildren.'[32]

Articles started appearing in local newspapers such as *The Argus*, the main Dundalk newspaper, which carried the headline 'Equality bus rolls into town to urge yes vote in referendum'.[33] The article became typical of the media reports which began flooding local radio and newspapers. *The Argus* carried a striking picture of the bus flanked by the volunteers describing how 'the colourful bus attracted a large amount of interest and dozens of people visited the vehicle to show their support for marriage equality'.[34] As well as arriving at town centres, the bus went to key locations such as university campuses. When the Yes bus reached the University of Limerick a full account was released by the university's *College News* on 15 May. An added attraction for gaining media attention included local celebrities or politicians who showed up in their local towns to publicly support the Yes Equality campaign. Other national figures such as the Taoiseach, Enda Kenny, even joined the tour at one stage.

The Yes bus was an immense success. Healy, Sheehan and Whelan describe how the bus driver, Andy Wilkinson, 'a burly Scotsman living in Swords ... emerged as an unexpected hero'.[35] The bus was rented for the month-long campaign and the bus company supplied drivers. When he began the job, Wilkinson had not thought much about LGBT rights and he did not encounter many gay men or lesbians. Wilkinson spent a month driving the team around the country and he described this as life changing. He told the *Irish Times* how he wanted to see a Yes vote win, describing how 'the girls and boys on this bus get abuse on the street. They are so polite, but I have seen them walking back and crying. Anyone who saw that would change their minds. I have.'[36]

The No supporters were also building a more focused campaign. The main organisation promoting the No vote, as identified by Healy, Sheehan and Whelan, was the organisation Mothers and Fathers Matter.[37] As mentioned earlier, the group was established in September 2014, chaired by economist Professor Ray Kinsella, initially to oppose the Children and Family Relationships Bill; hence its title. The organisation extended its remit to oppose marriage equality. Its No vote campaign was launched in the central Dublin city hotel, the Davenport, a favoured venue for Iona Institute gatherings. The launch followed a high-profile press conference at the venue on 17 April 2015.

When media representatives questioned MFM regarding the current opinion polls showing a Yes majority, their spokesperson, Keith Mills, said such polls were 'notoriously unreliable'.[38] Mills noted his belief that 'once the debates kick in then I think we will see the

Irish people supporting marriage and the family as it exists at the moment'.[39] Mills, himself an out gay man, was a prominent spokesperson for the No campaign. He had written a detailed account entitled 'Why I'll be voting "No" to same-sex marriage, even though I'm gay' for the *Irish Independent* which was later published as a pamphlet to promote the No vote.[40] In it Mills maintained that 'in Ireland, we are very lucky that the people are being given the right to decide on whether marriage should be protected as it currently is, or be redefined at the behest of a tiny but vocal minority'.[41] Concluding that 'the small number of countries that have legalised same-sex marriage have done so without a vote and sometimes against public opinion, causing a great deal of resentment'.[42]

At that press conference a number of new faces emerged who would become prominent in the No campaign over the next number of weeks. Tom Finnegan, an advisor of MFM, described how they had already secured financial support. He quoted a funding target of €160,000, of which 80,000 had already achieved, but he feared being 'heavily outspent by the other side'.[43] Regardless of this concern, Healy, Sheehan and Whelan noted that within days of this launch MFM began putting up No campaign posters. Yes Equality estimated that 'Mothers and Fathers Matter had put up at least 30,000 posters. It was the most extensive postering campaign seen in Ireland outside a general election. At an estimated €10 per poster for materials, printing, erecting, take down and disposal.'[44]

There was a series of three posters as part of the MFM campaign. The first carried just text, with the slogans 'we already have civil partnerships: don't redefine marriage – Vote No'. The other two posters focused on children and families. One of these posters featured the image of a young girl under the heading 'Surrogacy?' The tag line here was 'she needs her mother for life, not just for 9 months'. This poster angered and upset a whole range of families across the country, well beyond families headed by same-sex couples. In an interview with the *Irish Independent*, a mother-of-two, Teresa Byrne, described how 'the poster is nonsense – it implies that surrogacy is simply for same-sex couples. There are many parents, myself included, that have had children thanks to the help of other people.'[45] Byrne continued by expressing the concerns of many people that 'to say that I am not the mother of my children because I could not biologically carry them is an insulting suggestion, and one that is clearly aimed at shaming families that do not conform to this group's narrow view of what constitutes a family'.[46]

The third poster became the most prominent one used by MFM; it featured a close-up shot of a man and a woman kissing the cheek of a baby. The image was clearly meant to represent the traditional image of a heterosexual family unit. The picture was positioned under a large heading announcing 'Children deserve a Mother and a Father.' The main slogan underneath was simply 'Vote No', alongside the logo of MFM. The posters attempted to confuse the basis of the upcoming referendum. A vote of No would be a vote against extending civil marriage to same-sex couples. The legal implications for the children of such relationships were not in question in the referendum – these issues were covered by the Children and Family Relationships Bill. The Chairman of MFM, Ray Kinsella, accused the government of 'acting with expediency, "purportedly taking children out of the equation", by enacting the Children and Family Relationships Bill before the referendum. "You can never take children out of the equation,"' he maintained.[47] Kinsella clearly intended the posters to bring the focus back to children. However, this would backfire spectacularly when on 7 May 2015, two weeks before the referendum, the family pictured in the most prominent poster released a public statement. It seemed the people pictured were in fact a family from the UK and were unaware that their stock image had been used in this way. The couple were deeply upset with the use of their image to support MFM's No campaign, an opinion with which they did not agree.

Through Amnesty International Ireland, the couple released a statement testifying that 'we completely support same-sex marriage, and we believe that same-sex couples should of course be able to adopt, as we believe that they are equally able to provide children with much-needed love and care. To suggest otherwise is offensive to us, and to many others.'[48] The couple continued by noting that 'discrimination on the grounds of sexuality has no place in the 21st century. If we were residents of Ireland, not the UK, we would vote Yes for marriage equality.'[49]

## Notes

1 'Wording of same-sex marriage referendum published', *RTÉ online edition* (21 January 2016), available at: www.rte.ie/news/2015/0121/674602-marriage-equality/ (accessed 2 July 2018).

2  Ibid.
3  Healy, Sheehan and Whelan, *Ireland Says Yes*, p. 33.
4  Referendum Commission, *Report on the Referendums on Marriage and on the Age of Presidential Candidates* (October 2015), p. 2.
5  Ibid., p. 5.
6  Ibid.
7  Ibid.
8  Belfast Telegraph Digital, 'Dublin priest receives standing ovation after saying he is gay during mass', *Belfast Telegraph* (9 January 2015), available at: www.belfasttelegraph.co.uk/news/republic-of-ireland/dublin-priest-receives-standing-ovation-after-saying-he-is-gay-during-mass-3089 4931.html (accessed 11 April 2017); Gary Meneely, 'Priest comes out at mass', *Irish Sun* (6 January 2015); Skibbereen Eagle Online, 'Blessed are the gays', *Skibbereen Eagle* (11 January 2015), available at: www.skibbereeneagle.ie/uncategorized/blessed-gays (accessed 11 April 2017).
9  Jamie Orme, *Guardian* (10 January 2015); Carol Kuruvilla, *The Huffington Post* (12 January 2015).
10 Patsy McGarry, 'Fr Iggy O'Donovan calls for Yes vote in marriage referendum', *Irish Times* (10 March 2015).
11 J. Lester Feder, 'There is a battle going on within the Irish Catholic Church at the moment', BuzzFeed News (18 May 2015), available at: www.buzzfeednews.com/article/lesterfeder/priests-defy-bishops-to-support-marriage-equality-in-ireland (accessed 6 September 2019).
12 Stephen Rogers, 'Priests' group will not make recommendation in marriage vote', *Irish Examiner* (25 March 2015).
13 Gaelic Athletic Association.
14 Fr John Britto, 'Full sermon of Fr. John Britto on same sex marriage', *Donegal Daily* (20 March 2015).
15 Ibid.
16 Órla Ryan, 'Church of Ireland won't be campaigning for same-sex marriage vote', *The Journal* (2 February 2015).
17 Michael O' Regan, 'Equality group urging Yes in marriage referendum launched', *Irish Times* (9 March 2015).
18 Charlie Bird, *One Day in May: Real lives, true stories*, Dublin, 2016.
19 George Hicks, 'Yes Equality campaign launched in Dublin', *Pink News* (9 March 2015).
20 Ibid.
21 Susan Parker, *The Path to Marriage Equality in Ireland: A case study* (2017), p. 11.
22 Ibid., p. 12.
23 Ibid.
24 The GPO on O'Connell Street. Since the Easter Rising of 1916, when

the GPO was used as the headquarters for an attack on British rule in Ireland, the landmark building has become an important site for Irish people to gather in protest or in celebration.

25 'Amnesty International launches Yes campaign for marriage equality' (10 March 2015), available at: www.amnesty.ie/amnesty-internation al-launches-yes-campaign-marriage-equality/ (accessed 4 July 2018).

26 Mary Minihan, 'Mothers and Fathers Matter launches No referendum campaign', *Irish Times* (17 April 2015).

27 Noel Whelan, 'Exhausting, draining and life changing: The Yes campaign', *Irish Times* (24 May 2015).

28 Parker, *Path to Marriage Equality*, p. 13.

29 Ibid., p. 12.

30 Healy, Sheehan and Whelan, *Ireland Says Yes*, p. 39.

31 Ibid., p. 40.

32 SIPTU, 'Yes Equality campaign takes to the road', SIPTU news release (22 April 2015), available at: www.siptu.ie/media/newsarchive2015/fullstory_19039_en.html (accessed 6 July 2018).

33 *The Argus* (29 April 2015).

34 Ibid.

35 Healy, Sheehan and Whelan, *Ireland Says Yes*, p. 93.

36 Anthea McTeirnan, 'On the road to somewhere: the bus driver's tale', *Irish Times* (20 May 2015).

37 Healy, Sheehan and Whelan, *Ireland Says Yes*, p. 116.

38 Minihan, 'Mothers and Fathers Matter'.

39 Ibid.

40 Keith Mills, 'Why I'll be voting "No" to same-sex marriage, even though I'm gay', *Irish Independent* (1 February 2015).

41 Ibid.

42 Ibid.

43 Minihan, 'Mothers and Fathers Matter'.

44 Healy, Sheehan and Whelan, *Ireland Says Yes*, p. 117.

45 David Kearns, 'Families hit out over "No" campaign poster criticising surrogacy', *Irish Independent* (23 April 2015).

46 Ibid.

47 Minihan, 'Mothers and Fathers Matter'.

48 Colm O'Gorman, 'Family in No poster says Yes to marriage equality in Ireland', Amnesty International Ireland (7 May 2015), available at: www.amnesty.org/en/latest/news/2015/05/family-in-no-poster-says-yes-to-marriage-equality-in-ireland/ (accessed 2 July 2018).

49 Ibid.

# 10

# The final hurdles

'Don't get Angry – Donate' was the Yes Equality response to the MFM poster campaign.[1] As Healy, Sheehan and Whelan explained, the No posters actually helped Yes Equality as they 'provoked many yes supporters out of their complacency'.[2] The call to donate or volunteer to canvass in those final weeks of the campaign was answered by many more people. The online donations fund increased overwhelmingly, with an average of €1,000 per hour being donated over the twenty-four hours after the No posters first appeared.[3] Likewise, the number of people volunteering to be involved in canvassing increased.

In the final month of the campaign many organisations, businesses and high-profile people came out in public support of a Yes vote. This was an immense boost to Yes Equality campaigners and drove them forward. The issue of children had become a central focus of the No campaign. This inspired Irish children's charities to openly join the debate. Barnardos, the Irish Society for the Prevention of Cruelty to Children and the Children's Rights Alliance joined forces in a public call for a Yes vote, which they declared would be 'in the best interest of children'. Speaking to the *Irish Times* a spokesperson explained this move was made because 'groups within the No campaign were using children ... as pawns and in a way that was dishonest'.[4]

A steady stream of Yes supporters emerged throughout May. On the first day of the month, Martin Shanhan, Head of IDA Ireland,[5] was forthright in his assertion to the *Irish Times* that 'a Yes vote on May 22 would tell the business world that Ireland is open, inclusive and welcomes diversity'. The newspaper carried the headline 'A yes vote is good for business'.[6] Days later, government Ministers headed numerous public endorsements. On 5 May, Leo Varadkar, as Minister for Health, joined forces with health professionals including doctors and nurses in the Yes for Health campaign. The group was supported by Aodhan O'Riordain, Labour Party Minister for New Communities, Culture and Equality; Liam Doran, General Secretary of the Irish Nurses and Midwives Organisation; and Kieran Ryan, CEO of the Irish College of General Practitioners.[7] Varadkar warned of the health implications of a No vote, which would be a 'big step backwards for the country, and ... would have an adverse effect on the mental health of members of the LGBT community'.[8] On 6 May, Fine Gael's Simon Coveney, then Minister for Defence, launched a Sports for Yes campaign. As part of Coveney's drive he featured in a video with Derval O'Rourke, Olympian gold medallist; Peter O'Mahony, Irish rugby union player; and Donal Óg Cusack, Cork hurler and all-Ireland winner, who all endorsed the Yes vote.[9] The day after, Ken Murphy, Director General of the Law Society of Ireland, announced that 'marriage equality is an issue of fundamental rights and there is no legal justification for denying equality to same-sex couples'.[10]

While such shows of public support were an immense boost to Yes Equality, another major obstacle to the campaign also appeared during this time. On the second day of May, the Irish Catholic Media Office released a statement from the Primate of All Ireland and Bishop of Armagh, Eamon Martin. The message was entitled 'Care for the covenant of marriage' and the text was preceded with Martin's main point: 'to interfere with the definition of marriage is not a simple or trivial matter'.[11] This message was to be conveyed to parishioners across Ireland at mass the next day (see appendix 1 for full text). Martin was forthright in his condemnation of marriage for same-sex couples and even of homosexual unions more broadly, referring to the Extraordinary Synod on the Family which met in Rome in 2014. Martin reiterated the conclusion of the Synod that 'there are absolutely no grounds for considering homosexual unions to be in any way similar or even remotely analogous to God's plan for marriage and family'.[12] Martin maintained that Irish people were now afraid to question the basis of marriage for same-sex couples for fear of being labelled homophobic. The statement was a resounding endorsement for the No campaign and came out of the blue for Yes Equality campaigners.

The initial report on RTÉ television regarding the archbishop's letter shocked Sheehan, who described how 'it was much more forceful than I would have imagined. They were clever enough not to ask people to vote yes or no because they would have had to register [as a campaign organisation], but they asked people to consider their vote carefully. They are brilliant media manipulators, and they released it so it would get on the 6 p.m. news on a Saturday evening so would dominate the airwaves for the next few days.'[13] The response to the Catholic Church needed to be carefully planned. Yes Equality issued an official statement regarding the archbishop's letter to accompany the piece on the 9pm RTÉ news the evening it was first announced. Cathy Madden, Noel Whelan, Healy and Sheehan prepared a response outlining their disappointment and invited the archbishop to meet with Yes Equality to have an open dialogue about the upcoming referendum. The invitation was followed up by Healy when she went on RTÉ the following Monday morning, again requesting dialogue with the archbishop. There was no response from the Catholic hierarchy.

Worse was to come – in response to Martin's statement, eight senior bishops in Ireland wrote their own pastoral letters to be read at mass. A highly organised press campaign by the Catholic hierarchy followed for the three weekend masses before the referendum. The Archbishop of Tuam, Michael Neary, warned that 'we should be aware of what is at stake here. We are in fact redefining the family. Throughout history and across all cultures, marriage has been consistently understood to be the union of male and female with procreative potential.'[14] The Bishop of Limerick, Brennan Leahy, put forward an unusual argument, suggesting that if marriage were extended to same-sex couples school books would have to be changed if they did not support such marriages. This argument had no grounding but seemed to stem from a similar claim put forward by anti-divorce advocates during the divorce referendum in 1995. The Archbishop of Dublin and Primate of Ireland, Diarmuid Martin, took a more measured approach. Martin vehemently opposed extending marriage to same-sex couples, but he did however acknowledge that civil partnerships needed to be improved.[15]

The bishops' letters were read out at mass over the final three weeks before the vote, and stories began to emerge of protests happening at churches around the country. The *Enniscorthy Guardian* reported how a letter by Bishop Denis Brennan urging people to vote No was read out during Saturday evening mass the week before the referendum. A number of people walked out, 'including some members of the choir'.[16] One woman who walked out of Enniscorthy Cathedral told the *Irish Independent*, 'it was nothing against Fr Lawless. He was only reading the letter. When he started speaking he talked about God and love and I thought it was going in the right direction and that they (the Church) were going to come into the 21st century, but then he read out the letter and I couldn't believe it. I couldn't in all conscience sit there and listen to it.'[17] Brennan's letter followed a similar line to the campaign led by MFM focusing on children; he noted that children have 'a natural right to a mother and a father. Sometimes, unfortunately due to circumstances beyond everybody's control this does not obtain, but this is quite different from legislating to make it impossible for some.'[18]

Yes Equality began to focus on Catholic priests and devout lay Catholics who supported Yes Equality and let them tell their stories. In this way, rather than generate a confrontation Yes Equality attempted to quash the Catholic hierarchy's message with positive messages. Tom Curran, Fine Gael General Secretary and a devout Catholic, went public about his personal story. On 9 May, in the pages of the *Irish Independent*, Curran announced, 'as a man of faith and a proud Dad to a gay son, I urge all Catholics to do the right thing – and vote yes'.[19] Curran, who described himself as a 'card-carrying Catholic', was involved in establishing the Association of Catholics of Ireland and was active in his local parish of Enfield/Rathmolyon, Diocese of Meath. He spoke openly about when his son, Finnian, came out as a gay man to him. The only concern for Curran and his wife Noeleen was the 'lovely life' they wanted for Finnian, 'including marriage'. He concluded by stating that 'I've come on a journey, in terms of my belief, and I feel comfortable in urging all people of faith to consider the equal marriage referendum seriously and to vote yes. In my view, it's the right thing – the moral thing – to do.'[20]

The biggest boost for the Yes Equality campaign in response to these stories from committed Catholics happened when, on 15 May, Ursula Halligan, a popular political editor at TV3 and a devoted Catholic, came out as a lesbian in an article she wrote for the *Irish Times* (see appendix 2 for the full article). The article gave an honest and heart-breaking account of how she realised that she was a lesbian when she was seventeen years old. As a Catholic in Ireland, Halligan described how she learnt to supress her feelings and hide her true self as 'homophobia was so deeply embedded in my soul, I resisted facing the truth about myself'.[21] The marriage equality campaign in Ireland became 'the game-changer' for her, and Halligan wrote that this led her 'toward the first option: telling the truth to anyone who cares. And I knew if I was going to tell the truth, I had to tell the whole truth and reveal my backing for a Yes vote. For me, the two are intrinsically linked.'[22]

Halligan had planned to come out about her sexuality earlier in the marriage equality campaign but she experienced a deep personal trauma in the weeks leading up to the referendum when her brother, Professor Aidan Halligan, died suddenly. Now Halligan told her story one week before the referendum. She was clear about what a Yes vote would mean to her and to gay and lesbian people in Ireland:

> It will end institutional homophobia. It will say to gay people that they belong, that it's safe to surface and live fully human, loving lives. If it's true that 10 per cent of any population are gay, then there could be 400,000 gay people out there; many of them still living in emotional prisons. Any of them could be your son, daughter, brother, sister, mother, father or best friend. Set them free. Allow them [to] live full lives.

The month of May also meant three weeks of intense media debate as the referendum drew nearer. This included *The Late Late Show* on 1 May, which set up a traditional political-style debate programme. Representatives from both sides were interviewed individually by programme host Ryan Tubridy and then made their opening statements at a podium before a full debate ensued. Colm O'Gorman and journalist Una Mullally represented the Yes campaign. Keith Mills and Petra Conroy, Co-ordinator of Catholic Comment, a group of Catholic public commentators, represented the No campaign. It was soon realised that such appearances were central to the final stages of the referendum, in order to sway undecided voters at the very least. Yes Equality decided to elect what it described as 'its own identifiable voice'.[23] It was agreed to nominate Healy as the female voice in upcoming debates while Sheehan would speak on campaign matters. However, this campaign was one for equality, not just for LGBT people, and therefore it was vitally important to also have heterosexual spokespeople. Noel Whelan seemed the obvious choice and it appears that the media sought him out for this role.[24] The No campaign, represented mainly by MFM and the Iona Institute, adopted a similar process and its main spokespeople emerged in the final weeks: David Quinn, Director of the Iona Institute; and solicitor Eileen King and journalist John Waters, both of MFM.

The same day that Ursula Halligan's article appeared in the *Irish Times*, a group of senior lawyers, backed by the Iona Institute, issued a statement calling for a No vote. The group comprised three men: William Binchy, a prominent pro-life advocate, and two senior counsels; Patrick Treacy and Shane Murphy. In its statement, the group maintained that 'the marriage referendum is the next major step in a programme of social engineering which not just obscures our understanding of the human person as male and female (the new "gender theory") but which endorses the severing of the natural ties between a child and his or her biological parents. This radical programme has already begun with the enactment into law of the Children and Family Relationships Act, 2015 on April 6th, 2015.'[25] They concluded that 'same-sex marriage is not a human right', referring to a statement by former President Mary McAleese, a stalwart supporter of LGBT rights and marriage equality, to support this. The group claimed that 'Mary McAleese, did not say it is a human right. She said it is "a human rights issue."'[26]

Leaders of Yes Equality took a step back and assessed their next move, which they decided must be to 'respond forcefully to misleading information ... [T]hey held a press conference on May 15 to rebut the accusations made by the No side about the danger gay marriage posed for children.'[27] Justin McAleese, the son of Mary and Martin McAleese, put forward an astute idea to retaliate to MFM, which he called 'Fathers for Yes'. On Saturday 16 May, the Yes Equality National Canvas Day was launched at the GPO, where over four hundred volunteers had gathered. Three fathers – Tom Curran, Ashok Varadkar and Martin McAleese – stood in front of the GPO in support of their gay sons. Healy described this as 'the most poignant and memorable moment of the campaign. Watching these three quiet and dignified men standing up for their gay sons in front of the site of the birth of the Republic was astounding.'[28] The image of the men was captured and distributed to the main media across the country.

Also on 15 May it was discovered that 65,911 people had been included on the supplementary register for the referendum – this high number was a good indicator that turnout for the vote would be high and this in turn was good news for Yes Equality.[29] As the debates intensified and the numbers of polls estimating the outcome of the referendum increased, the importance of every possible vote grew. Pollsters indicated that the young voter would return a Yes vote. An early RED C opinion poll in 2014 indicated that as much as 88 per cent of 18–24-year-olds would vote Yes.[30] However, a large portion of this group had recently emigrated. Over the last two centuries, Ireland has been a country blighted by large patterns of emigration due to famine, political turbulence or economic necessity. During what became known as the Celtic Tiger, Ireland experienced a financial boom, especially during the decade from 1997–2007, which resulted in immigration greater than ever before experienced. Unfortunately, the following year an economic downturn began and many of those immigrants left Ireland along with a host of Irish-born citizens; emigration trebled between 2008 and 2012. The Central Statistics Office shows that in one year from April 2014 to April 2015, the year up to the referendum, 81,000 people left the country.[31] A study by the Migration Policy Institute testifies that this figure 'exceeds even the highest rates of emigration in the 1950s and 1980s'.[32]

The emigrant vote was important but also problematic. 'Ireland trails behind the rest of Europe – and many countries worldwide – in its attitude toward emigrant voting. Progress on voting rights in Ireland has been slow and, heretofore, ultimately unsuccessful.'[33] Definitively, any Irish citizen who leaves Ireland forfeits their entitlement to vote after eighteen months out of the country.[34] There are only very limited circumstances in which people can receive a postal vote; therefore any Irish citizen living outside the State would need to return home to a polling station to exercise their vote, within that eighteen-month period. Estimates maintained that at least 60,000 emigrants were still entitled to vote in the 2015 referendum but the financial cost to individuals could be enormous. If emigrants returned to vote this would mean taking time off work and paying for travel back to their home polling station. Numerous bills and proposals to include the emigrant voice in the running of their home country had failed over the recent past. Previous elections and referendums had not targeted the emigrant vote.

Months before the referendum took place campaigns such as 'We're Coming Back' began to emerge online, advocating for voting rights for Irish citizens abroad. Such groups were drawing attention and gaining increased numbers of members before the referendum date was called. In February 2015, three Irish emigrants – David Burns, then living in Paris; Conor O'Neil, then living in Brussels; and Joey Kavanagh, then living in London – founded an online campaign 'Get the Boat to Vote'. No one could have predicted that this would result in a mass movement of returning emigrants arriving in Ireland for the referendum vote on 22 May 2015. The movement, which used the hashtag #HomeToVote, went viral in the days before and the day of the referendum. By the time polls closed that night, more than 72,000 #HomeToVote mentions had been posted across Twitter. For those who could not afford the time off work or the cost of travel the hashtag #BeMyYes emerged, as Irish immigrants who could not vote implored others in Ireland to use their votes to register a Yes. This group described themselves as 'an online campaign to give a voice to those Irish abroad who cannot vote in Ireland's Marriage Equality Referendum'.[35]

As Brian Sheehan and Gráinne Healy closed down the campaign and thanked all the staff and volunteers at the Clarendon Street office the night before the referendum, Yvonne Judge asked them to look at her computer screen. The latest clip on the #HomeToVote hashtag was a video of Oonagh Murphy, one of the organisers of the initiative, leading a large group of emigrants from London back home to Dublin on board the ferry.[36] As the boat pulled in to Dublin harbour the song 'She Moves Through the Fair' echoed across the group. 'It will not be long now till our wedding day.'

## Notes

1  Healy, Sheehan and Whelan, *Ireland Says Yes*, p. 121.
2  Ibid., p. 121.
3  Ibid.
4  Kitty Holland, 'Children's charities call for a Yes in same-sex marriage vote', *Irish Times* (29 April 2015).
5  The Industrial Development Authority, a semi-State body responsible for attracting foreign direct investment into the country.
6  Arthur Beesley, *Irish Times* (1 May 2015).
7  Lise Hand, 'Leo Varadkar calls for a Yes vote in marriage equality referendum', *Irish Independent* (5 May 2015).

8   Ibid.

9   Ralph Riegel and Ryan Nugent, 'Sports stars and women's groups back Yes campaign', *Irish Independent* (6 May 2015).

10  Fiona Gartland, 'Marriage equality is a human right, says Law Society', *Irish Times* (7 May 2015).

11  Archbishop Eamon Martin, *Care for the Covenant of Marriage*, Irish Catholic Media Office (2 May 2015).

12  Ibid.

13  Parker, *Path to Marriage Equality*, p. 14.

14  Nicky Ryan, 'Catholic leaders are out in force arguing against same-sex marriage', *The Journal* (10 May 2015).

15  Ibid.

16  *Enniscorthy Guardian* as cited in Esther Hayden, ' "Walk-out" during mass at cathedral over letter from bishop', *Irish Independent* (16 May 2015).

17  Ibid.

18  Ibid.

19  Tom Curran, *Irish Independent* (9 May 2015).

20  Ibid.

21  Ursula Halligan, 'Referendum led me to tell the truth about myself', *Irish Times* (15 May 2015).

22  Ibid.

23  As noted in Healy, Sheehan and Whelan, *Ireland Says Yes*, p. 127.

24  Ibid.

25  Patrick Treacy SC, Shane Murphy SC, William Binchy, 'Senior lawyers urge no vote in marriage referendum', Iona Institute for Religion and Society website (15 May 2015), available at: https://ionainstitute.ie/senior-lawyers-urge-no-vote-in-marriage-referendum/ (accessed 10 July 2018).

26  Ibid.

27  Parker, *Path to Marriage Equality*, p. 15.

28  Healy, Sheehan and Whelan, *Ireland Says Yes*, p. 145.

29  Ibid., p. 142.

30  RED C, 'Same sex marriage opinion poll', *Sunday Business Post* and RTÉ (20 February 2014).

31  Central Statistics Office, 'Population and migration 2015', as cited in Irial Glynn with Tomás and Piaras Mac Éinrí, *The Re-emergence of Emigration from Ireland: New trends in an old story* (Washington DC: Migration Policy Institute, 2015), p. 5.

32  Irial Glynn with Tomás and Piaras Mac Éinrí, *The Re-emergence of Emigration from Ireland: New trends in an old story*, Washington DC, 2015, p. 5.

33  Ibid., p. 17.

34  Section 5 (4) of the Electoral Act 1963 stipulates that Irish citizens overseas are entitled to vote for up to eighteen months after they leave.

35  The BeMyYes campaign operated online mainly through its Facebook site, available at: www.facebook.com/pg/bemyyes/about/?ref=page_internal (accessed 5 July 2018).

36  Healy, Sheehan and Whelan, *Ireland Says Yes*, p. 162.

# 11

# The referendum

The polling stations opened at 7am on Friday 22 May 2015. Voters turned out in their droves to vote on the proposed thirty-fourth and thirty-fifth Amendments to the Irish Constitution. Polling stations remained open for fifteen hours and in that time nearly two million people arrived to have their say.[1] Voting turnout was remarkably high for a referendum, with 60.52 per cent of those entitled to vote showing up at polling stations around the country. This was in fact the highest recorded turnout since November 1995, when 62.2 per cent turnout was recorded for the divorce referendum. Since the 1970s, it had not been unusual for turnout percentage to be as low as in the 20s or 30s at referendums in Ireland. The referendum directly prior to this in 2013 on the questions of abolishing the Seanad and mandating a new court of appeal saw less than 40 per cent turnout. The marriage equality referendum reversed the trend of decreasing voter turnout.

The Yes Equality team had concerns before the count got underway. Three different polls on 17 May indicated a majority Yes. This did not assure campaign leaders. The 1995 divorce referendum polls had also shown a large majority Yes vote before polling day. However, divorce only passed in Ireland by a 0.6 per cent majority, with 50.3 per cent for and 49.7 per cent voting against. Polls are not always accurate. Added to this, there was the issue of the so-called 'shy No' vote. In his assessment of the data results, consultant Matthew Isbell describes how 'the issue of a "shy no" voter came from the fact that the YES campaign used a very emotional and effective narrative to persuade people to vote Yes. The concern was that opponents of the measure would have feared being labelled intolerant or homophobic, and thus kept their opposition to themselves.'[2]

The count started at 9am on Saturday 23 May. It was instantly evident that this was a unique referendum as people lined the streets queueing to get into vote centres. The Royal Dublin Society (RDS) count centre proved to be a popular choice for people wanting to help Yes Equality by tallying votes. At 9.14am the *Irish Times* live coverage announced, 'strong indications from a reputable (neutral) source that early indications from Dublin North are that it's 65 to 70 per cent Yes there'.[3] Soon similar reports from around the country began to emerge. At 9.33am, the first box opened and counted in Carrick-on-Suir recorded a 77–23 vote in favour of Yes. At 10am, David Quinn of the Iona Institute and MFM conceded defeat when he tweeted 'Congratulations to the Yes side. Well done. #MarRef.' The Yes result tallies seemed to increase as counting continued. By 10.19am, fifty boxes opened in Wicklow showed Yes results of Arklow 63 per cent, Bray 73 per cent, Greystones 74 per cent and Wicklow Town 71 per cent. For the remainder of the day reporting focused not on whether a Yes vote won in a constituency but by how much and which area had the highest recorded Yes vote. Una Mullally tweeted at 10.57am, 'we have a new highest Yes vote in the country: Ranelagh 84.4 per cent.' Social media was awash with congratulations to Ireland from around the world. J. K Rowling tweeted at 11.15am: 'sitting here watching the Irish make history. Extraordinary and wonderful.'

The excitement throughout the morning had built into almost a frenzy by lunchtime. The upper courtyard of Dublin Castle was open for the public to gather and watch the count unfold on big screens, while a stage was erected where campaigners, activists, politicians and celebrities who supported Yes Equality took position. Panti Bliss arrived on the scene just before 3pm to an almighty welcome from thousands gathered in the old cobbled courtyard. David Norris described how Ireland was now an example to the rest of the world. Others on stage included Katherine Zappone and Anne Louise Gilligan; Una Mullally; Gerry Adams; Eamon Gilmore; Enda Kenny; Joan Burton; and Leo Varadkar, to name but a few. As the results confirming Yes in every constituency streamed in, the emotional celebrations reached a high by early afternoon. The only shadow was at just before 5pm, when the Roscommon-South

Leitrim result was announced as a No majority of 51.42 per cent to 48.58 per cent Yes. This was the only constituency across the entire twenty-six counties of Ireland that registered a No majority.

Unfortunately, the reputation of the constituency came under attack as the only area with a No majority vote. However, as *The Journal* pointed out, 'all of this criticism comes despite the fact that more people voted Yes in Roscommon-South Leitrim (17,615) than in both Donegal North-East (16,040) and Donegal South-West (15,907) and that fewer people voted No in Roscommon-South Leitrim than in 13 constituencies.'[4] Indeed, in recognition of this Kieran Rose later acknowledged the 'fantastic' work done by Yes campaigners in the constituency. The campaigners in Roscommon-Leitrim were clearly disappointed and posted on their Facebook page:

> Unfortunately, we were small in number, and did not have the human resources to do, for example, large scale canvasses as seen in other areas. We also suffered from a lack of support from local politicians. We watched in envy as well known politicians in almost every other area in the country got publicly and deeply involved in the campaigns in their areas. Our multiple letters, texts and emails to our elected representatives went, for the most part, unanswered.[5]

News of the overall results swept across the globe during the count day. The *New York Times*, released at 5pm Irish time, headlined with 'Ireland appears set to legalize gay marriage by popular vote'. Just before 7pm the final result was officially announced, declaring a Yes majority by nearly half a million votes (467,307). The highest recorded constituency with a Yes vote was in Dublin South East, which returned nearly 75 per cent Yes. The total poll was 1,949,725, with valid votes after spoilt ballots coming in at 1,935,907. This was a truly historic moment. Ireland would be the first country ever to extend marriage to same-sex couples through a public vote.

In his assessment of the campaign data, Isbell highlighted numerous reasons why a small, Catholic, conservative country such as Ireland had voted overwhelmingly Yes to marriage equality. He praised the campaign, which managed to receive 'a significantly larger amount of institutional support compared to the No side. All of the major political parties came out for the measure, including the Incumbent Prime Minister and the former President.'[6] This was a unique aspect of this campaign. Support crossed all party thresholds. A *Sunday*

*Times* poll measured support for marriage equality by party allegiance and while all party followers were in favour of a Yes vote, the level of support radically differed across parties, showing as 100 per cent Yes support for Green Party followers as opposed to a narrow margin of 53 per cent for Fianna Fáil disciples.

There was a fall-out for the Fianna Fáil party after the referendum results were formally announced. Senator Averil Power quit Fianna Fáil, signalling that the party had not been supportive of her or of the drive to obtain full marriage equality in Ireland. In a statement released just two days after the vote was tallied, Power described how Fianna Fáil's 'cynical and cowardly approach to the marriage equality referendum was the last straw' for her. She went on to note that 'for me, a referendum on equality went to the core of what real republicanism should be about. Our members knew that when they voted for a motion calling for the party to support marriage equality at the 2012 Ard Fheis.'[7]

For Isbell, as for many other political commentators, it was the personal stories of the Yes Equality campaign that had the most power in swaying undecided voters to opt for Yes. The No campaign's negative tactics, seen through MFM and the Catholic hierarchy's messages, backfired immensely. In his report Isbell notes that, 'the YES campaigns worked hard to evoke emotion in the debate, running powerful ads and using personal stories to pull at the heart-strings of the voters. The NO campaigners tried to argue the family would be damaged by the measure.'[8] Globally Ireland is viewed as a primarily Catholic country and indeed in 2011, in the last recorded census of the population before this referendum, 84 per cent of the population identified as Catholic. This may be related to the pressure among Irish populations to be baptised, especially in order to gain entry into local schools which are predominantly Catholic. However, the number of practising Catholics in the country is rapidly declining, especially since the late 1990s. The decline in church attendance is undoubtedly connected to priest child abuse scandals and the mistreatment of women in Mother and Baby homes which have affected Ireland particularly.

While Yes Equality leaders had been surprised and disappointed at the archbishops' and bishops' messages to their congregations regarding the referendum, these were in fact, as Isbell describes, 'tepid' in comparison to previous referendums on social issues.[9] This soft approach was in direct response to calls by Church officials for civility during the referendum campaign and an awareness that expressions of homophobia are un-Christian. This approach and the fact that many Catholic leaders came out in support of a Yes vote greatly helped the cause. As well as priests and respected members of the Catholic lay community already mentioned, other Catholic community leaders publicly declared that they would be voting Yes. Sister Stanislaus Kennedy (Sr Stan), founder of Focus Ireland, stated that 'I am going to vote Yes in recognition of the gay community as full members of society. They should have an entitlement to marry. It is a civil right and a human right.' [10] Fr Peter McVerry, a lifelong advocate of the homeless and founder of the Peter McVerry Trust, explained that 'I think we ought to recognise the love that exists between two people of the same sex; that's not a problem for me. It's essentially a civil matter that marriage is being regulated by the state and I don't think the church should impose its own moral code on people who may not believe it.' [11] These leaders are more respected in Irish communities than the hierarchy of the Catholic Church and such testimonies had a greater impact on voter activity.

When interviewed immediately following the final result of the referendum on 23 May, Archbishop Diarmuid Martin admitted that the results showed how the 'Catholic Church needs a reality check in the wake of the same-sex marriage referendum and needs to ask if it has drifted away from young people'. [12] The response from the Vatican was less reflective. The Secretary of State for the Vatican, Cardinal Pietro Parolin, considered second in command to the Pope, issued a statement at a conference in Rome. Parolin agreed 'the church must take account of this reality'; however, he continued to explain that 'it must strengthen its commitment to evangelisation. I think you cannot just talk of defeat for Christian principles, but of a defeat for humanity.' [13]

The political reaction globally was extremely positive. Ban Ki-moon, then United Nations Secretary General, described how the result would send 'an important message to the world: All people are entitled to enjoy their human rights no matter who they are or whom they love.' He continued by praising Irish voters 'for making history in becoming the first country in the world to approve marriage equality in a nationwide referendum'. [14] Indeed, campaigners and politicians in countries which had yet to secure marriage equal-

Commission, argued that the referendum was passed by the Irish people with a "thumping majority" … [which] has been identified by the Supreme Court as a fact that can be considered significant'.[21] Both Walshe and Lyons had already requested an adjournment to assess the response by the State. In this instance Kearns was forthright as to the urgency of passing this law, describing how 'there could be couples with serious illnesses with plans that could be put on hold'. Both Walshe and Lyons appealed the High Court decision to dismiss their petitions and the appeal trial held on 30 July upheld the case dismissal.

On 24 August, Ní Fhlanghaile was officially notified by the High Court's Master that it had not accepted any petition against the referendum result. In turn Ní Fhlanghaile submitted the final certificate of the referendum results to both the President and the Taoiseach. Walshe and Lyons issued a further appeal to the Supreme Court on 27 August. This appeal could not prevent the process and President Michael D. Higgins signed the amendment into law two days later, on 29 August. It had been hoped that the law could have been passed through the Dáil before summer recess but this was not possible due to the petitions and appeals by Walshe and Lyons. The Marriage Bill 2015 could not be presented to the Dáil until it resumed on 22 September. The bill had already been passed by the cabinet at a special meeting on 16 September and it finally passed all necessary stages on 22 October. The Marriage Act 2015 extending civil marriage to same-sex couples in Ireland came into effect on 16 November. The following day Richard Dowlin and Cormac Gollogly were married in Tipperary, making history as the first same-sex Irish couple to be legally married in the Irish State.[22]

## Notes

1  1,949,725 people.
2  Matthew Isbell, 'The numbers behind Ireland's historic vote on same-sex marriage', *MCI Maps* (26 May 2015), available at: http://mcimaps.com/the-numbers-behind-irelands-historic-vote-on-same-sex-marriage/ (accessed 11 July 2018).
3  Dan Griffin, 'The counts – Ireland votes Yes', *Irish Times* (23 May 2015).
4  Christina Finn, 'Why did Roscommon-South Leitrim vote No?', *The Journal* (24 May 2015).

5  Yes Equality Roscommon official Facebook page (24 May 2015), available at: www.facebook.com/roscommonforequality/posts/183082415714 2128 accessed 13 July 2018 (accessed 13 July 2018).

6  Isbell, 'Numbers behind'.

7  Averil Power, 'Statement by Senator Averil Power on resigning from Fianna Fáil' (25 May 2015), available at: https://static.rasset.ie/docum ents/news/statement-by-senator-averil-power-on-resigning-from-fian na-fail.pdf (accessed 13 July 2018).

8  Isbell, 'Numbers behind'.

9  Ibid.

10  Carl O'Brien, 'Sr Stan to vote in favour of same sex marriage', *Irish Times* (11 May 2015).

11  Emily Dugan, 'Ireland's same-sex marriage vote: as date looms, the Irish ask – how would God vote?', *Independent UK* (20 May 2015).

12  Alison Healy, 'Diarmuid Martin: Catholic Church needs reality check', *Irish Times* (23 May 2015).

13  Stephanie Kirchgaessner, 'Vatican says Ireland gay marriage vote is "defeat for humanity"', *Guardian* (26 May 2015).

14  Carty and Baker, 'Ban Ki-moon praises Ireland'.

15  Derek Scally, 'Angela Merkel urged to follow Ireland's lead on same-sex marriage', *Irish Times* (24 May 2015).

16  'Gay marriage referendum in Australia dismissed by Tony Abbott', *ABC News* (24 May 2015).

17  Claire Cromie, 'Gay marriage now has overwhelming support in Northern Ireland – poll', *Belfast Telegraph* (6 July 2015).

18  Rónán Duffy, '"A thumping majority" – High Court rejects two legal challenges to marriage referendum', *The Journal* (5 June 2015).

19  Ibid.

20  Ibid.

21  Ibid.

22  David Kearns, 'Ireland's first same sex marriage takes place in Tipperary', *Irish Independent* (17 November 2015).

# Afterword: Future directions

In the final six weeks of 2015, ninety-one same-sex couples were legally married in Ireland. Forty-seven male couples and forty-four female couples were finally able to have their relationships legally recognised. The following year the Central Statistics Office compiled a full year of recorded marriages. In 2016, out of a total of 22,626 marriages in Ireland 1,056 were marriages by same-sex couples, accounting for almost one in twenty of all marriages, or 4.7 per cent. Civil ceremonies were the most popular route, with over 80 per cent of same-sex couples choosing this option. Other options included ceremonies by the Humanist Association of Ireland and the Spiritualist Union of Ireland. This was the main difference between same-sex and opposite-sex marriages. Sixty-seven per cent of opposite-sex marriages in Ireland took place by religious ceremony, with over half of all those marriages being Catholic ceremonies. Another notable difference is geographical. Nearly half of all marriages between same-sex couples took place in the capital city. In 2017, the number of marriages by same-sex couples fell to 759: 424 male unions and 335 female unions.[1]

The Children and Family Relationship Bill had been introduced in 2015, before the referendum, to ensure that children of same-sex couples would be legally protected within their family unit. Civil marriage should have been the final legal step for such families to be on an equal footing with families headed by opposite-sex couples. However, a 'typographical and technical error' in the original text of the act meant that Parts 2 and 3 could not be effectively introduced.[2] A cause for concern had been pointed out by Dr Brian Tobin in 2016, when he noted 'the State's failure to commence the relevant provisions of the Children and Family Relationships Act 2015'.[3]

Therefore, major issues remained for same-sex-parented families. Three years after the original bill was enacted an amendment bill was required. The Children and Family Relationships (Amendment) Act 2018 went through the parliamentary system, including amendments which are often particularly relevant to families of same-sex couples. The three main issues affected by the 'typographical and technical error' were related to parental rights of children born through surrogacy; the position of spouses of those availing of donor-assisted human reproduction outside the State; and to ensure that both same-sex parents are recorded on their children's birth certificates and any other legal documents.

The Children and Family Relationships (Amendment) Bill 2018 was entered for debate in the Dáil on 11 July 2018. In her summary of the required changes, People Before Profit TD, Ruth Coppinger addressed the issue of a three-year delay in introducing these momentous changes:

> LGBT+ people were hugely validated and affirmed by the majority of people in the marriage equality referendum. It has been shocking that we have not dealt adequately with the practicalities of their lives and made them fully equal families and people in society ... The delays that people have had to endure for the past three years are not acceptable. This is about children's rights and no matter who their parents are or how they came into the world they should have the same rights as anybody else. I have mentioned some of the key problems of inheritance, citizenship, leaving the country, getting passports and also parents not feeling that they, themselves, are registered and recognised as the parents of these children.[4]

The amendment bill later went through the Seanad and was passed by both Houses of the Oireachtas on 18 July 2018. The Minister for Health, Simon Harris, welcomed the passing of the Act and in a press release he 're-iterated his commitment to commence Parts 2 & 3 of the Children and Family Relationships Act 2015 as soon as possible in the autumn'.[5]

By August 2018, same-sex couples in the Republic of Ireland were well on their way to having full equality with marriages and family units headed by opposite-sex couples. However, the situation was far from resolved on the remainder of the island. The six counties in the North of Ireland had still not extended marriage to same-sex couples by this time. When the Irish referendum took place, Members of the Legislative Assembly (MLAs) had already voted on the issue of extending civil marriage to same-sex couples on four separate occasions at Stormont; on each occasion the majority voted against the legal change required. In June 2013, the bill to extend marriage to same-sex couples had been introduced to Westminster and the Northern Ireland Assembly had met to vote on how that bill should be received in their jurisdiction. The Assembly voted again to block introduction of marriage equality and this time included 'a legislative consent motion which excluded most of the provisions of the bill' then being passed through Westminster.[6] In this way the MLAs voted to recognise only civil partnerships for same-sex couples, even relating to couples who were legally married in the UK or elsewhere and moved to live in Northern Ireland.

The law extending marriage to same-sex couples had come into effect in England and Wales on 29 March 2014. On 29 April, a third attempt was made to pass a bill in the Northern Ireland Assembly. The vote lost by 51 against to 43 in favour. Opposition once again came predominantly from unionist parties, including the DUP, Ulster Unionist Party and Traditional Unionist Voice, with all nationalist MLAs voting in support of marriage equality. In the midst of these debates, Gareth Lee, a gay rights activist, was organising an event in Bangor, Co. Down to mark International Day Against Homophobia and Transphobia. As part of the celebrations, Lee ordered a cake made with the slogan 'support gay marriage' alongside an image of Bert and Ernie from Sesame Street and the logo of a gay rights group, Queer Space. Lee ordered the cake at Ashers Bakery in Belfast. When the order was sent to the headquarters of the evangelical Christian-owned bakery, they refused to fill the order. The grounds of the refusal were later explained by General Manager, Daniel McArthur, who stressed that 'we happily serve everyone but we cannot promote a cause that goes against what the Bible says about marriage. We have tried to be guided in our actions by our Christian beliefs.'[7]

The gay cake row, as it became known, apparently confused the issue of equality legislation and the introduction of marriage equality for same-sex couples. Although at the time the cake was ordered, marriage was not legal for same-sex couples in Northern Ireland, neither was it legal to deny goods or services to anyone based on grounds of equality legislation. Lee, supported by Northern Ireland's

Equality Commission, lodged a legal complaint which resulted in a trial that he won. The bakery was ordered to pay Lee £500 in damages. The case was far from over and continued for four and a half years alongside the complex and unsure future of marriage equality in Northern Ireland. Ashers appealed the court decision, which was rejected in 2016, and they sought a hearing in the Supreme Court, in which they were financially supported by the Christian Institute. The case was heard by five judges of the Supreme Court: Lady Hale, Lord Mance, Lord Kerr, Lord Hodge and Lady Black.[8] The court ruled in Ashers favour, overturning the initial judgment of 2014. In October 2018 the judgment was announced, with Lady Hale summarising the findings that 'freedom of expression, as guaranteed by article 10 of the European convention on human rights, includes the right "not to express an opinion which one does not hold" … this court has held that nobody should be forced to have or express a political opinion in which he does not believe'.[9] The cases cost the Equality Commission in Northern Ireland £250,000 in legal costs.

The gay cake row highlights the complexity of the political situation in Northern Ireland which has ultimately delayed the introduction of marriage equality there. A fourth attempt to introduce marriage equality was again voted down on 27 April 2015, in the weeks before the referendum in the South. This time the vote lost by a tighter margin of 49–47, again with unionist members being the main objectors. The political resistance, shown most obviously by the DUP, is however not representative of the position of the people of Northern Ireland. In the wake of the referendum, Ipsos MORI conducted a poll identifying that 68 per cent of people in the North of Ireland were in support of extending marriage to same-sex couples. This result was broken down by religion, showing 75 per cent of Catholics and 57 per cent of Protestants supporting marriage equality. The religious difference is undoubtedly related to support of political parties in Northern Ireland. The poll showed that 80 per cent of Sinn Féin supporters were in favour of marriage equality, while only 45 per cent of DUP voters were.[10] The DUP has close links with the Protestant Church, most evident from the fact that the Free Presbyterian Church of Ulster was established by DUP founder Ian Paisley.

No sooner did the celebrations of the referendum results in the Republic of Ireland die down than a new challenge to the laws in

Northern Ireland emerged. A case was put forward by two same-sex couples in Northern Ireland: Gráinne Close and Shannon Sickles along with Chris and Henry Flanagan-Kane. Gráinne and Shannon were the first same-sex couple to avail of a civil partnership in the UK at a ceremony held in the grounds of Belfast City Hall on 19 December 2005. They were followed by Chris and Henry, who were civil partnered later that day also in Northern Ireland. On 26 June 2015, both couples lodged a judicial review of the ban on marriage equality. Their barrister, Laura McMahon, argued that this was 'a fundamental discrimination of … rights under the European convention on human rights, which is without justification'.[11]

Meanwhile pressure mounted for the Northern Ireland Assembly to put the issue forward to another vote. Such a positive referendum result in the South of Ireland inevitably led to numerous public calls for extending marriage equality across the entire island. A fifth vote went through Stormont in November 2015 and this time a slim majority of MLAs voted in favour of introducing marriage equality, by 50.5 per cent. This was described as a 'symbolic victory by campaigners', as the DUP had tabled a 'petition of concern' at the start of the debate.[12] The petition of concern is best described by political analyst Claire Smyth, as a 'mechanism, which was introduced after the Good Friday Agreement in 1998 … and is meant to ensure that contentious legislation can only be introduced with cross-community support'.[13] Accordingly, the petition of concern was set in place in order to help the power-sharing government established through the Good Friday Agreement. The use of this petition to stop the introduction of marriage equality is seen by some, including Patrick Corrigan of Amnesty International NI, as an abuse of the system. Corrigan described it as 'misuse of the petition of concern to hold back rather than uphold the rights of a minority group'.[14]

Then First Minister to Northern Ireland and DUP leader, Arlene Foster made a commitment in October 2016 that her party would continue to block the introduction of marriage for same-sex couples for the next five years. It appeared that the only way change could be introduced was through ongoing legal challenges. However, in August 2017 Mr Justice O'Hara rejected the case put forward by Sickles, Close and the Flanagan-Kanes at the High Court. Their case was dismissed along with a further case originally lodged in January 2015. The other case, referred to as petition X as the couple sought anonymity, was lodged by a gay couple who married in London in 2014. The couple now live in Northern Ireland and wanted to have their marriage recognised there. The petition X case was supported by the Rainbow Project, whose Director, John O'Doherty, explained why the group was keen to support the legal challenge, attesting that 'while same-sex marriage legislation in Westminster had many positive aspects, we believe that its provision forbidding the recognition of lawful same-sex marriages in Northern Ireland is irrational, contrary to principles of British constitutional law and incompatible with the European Convention on Human Rights'.[15] The judge in his summary decided that it was not for the courts to decide on such issues but for the Stormont Assembly. Mr Justice O'Hara concluded, 'it is not at all difficult to understand how gay men and lesbians who have suffered discrimination, rejection and exclusion feel so strongly about the maintenance in Northern Ireland of the barrier to same sex marriage … However, the judgment which I have to reach is not based on social policy but on the law.'[16]

The couple in the case of petition X appealed this decision and they were supported by the Rainbow Project in Northern Ireland. The appeal case was heard by three judges under Lord Chief Justice Sir Declan Morgan. The judgment was reserved in March 2018, with an announcement originally scheduled for 2019. This, amid the collapse of Stormont, the Northern Ireland Assembly, in January 2017, left the future of marriage equality in Northern Ireland uncertain. The collapse of the power-sharing assembly means there have been no devolved Ministers in Northern Ireland since March 2017 and Stormont's government departments are being led by senior civil servants. Meanwhile the DUP entered government with the Conservative Party after the general election in June 2017 resulted in a hung Parliament.

At a Belfast Pride event on 30 July 2018, Sinn Féin leader, Mary Lou McDonald called on Westminster to break the current ban on marriage for same-sex couples in Northern Ireland.[17] A march had just been held calling for the introduction of marriage equality in Northern Ireland. The march, on 2 June 2018, saw over twenty thousand people turning up in support. Yes Equality activists continue to inspire activity in the North and speakers including Ailbhe Smyth addressed the gathered crowds on the streets of Belfast in June. Love Equality NI has now been established along the same lines as Yes

Equality. The group is a conglomerate of organisations advocating the extension of marriage to same-sex couples. These include Amnesty International NI, The Rainbow Project, Irish Congress of Trade Unions NI, Here NI, Cara-Friend and NUS–USI.[18] Love Equality – Campaign for Civil Marriage Equality in Northern Ireland was founded in its present form in April 2016. The campaign follows the successes of Yes Equality and mirrors activities which were used to great effect in the South, such as telling personal stories. The hashtag #tellyourlovestory continues to inspire change and works towards introducing marriage equality across the entire island of Ireland.

On 18 April 2019 journalist Lyra McKee was shot and killed by the dissident IRA while she was observing and reporting on a riot in Derry. The murder was a senseless act and McKee was certainly not the intended target. As well as being a talented journalist, Lyra was an outspoken advocate for marriage equality in Northern Ireland; she was also in a long-term relationship with another woman, Sara Canning. In a moving eulogy it was revealed by her close friend, Stephen Lusty, that McKee had planned a romantic marriage proposal to Canning in the coming weeks during their planned trip to New York.[19] Leaders of political parties from nationalist and unionist sides, including Arlene Foster and Mary Lou McDonald, were in attendance at the funeral, as was the British Prime Minister, Theresa May, and the Irish Taoiseach, Leo Varadkar. While politicians from across all communities condemned McKee's murder, it was telling that even after hearing such an emotional account of Lyra and Sara's relationship and planned future, Arlene Foster could still not contemplate changing her stance against marriage equality.

In an interview in May 2019, Canning described how she spoke with Theresa May at Lyra's funeral when she told her that 'if politicians won't legislate for equal marriage at Stormont, then the prime minister should do it at Westminster'.[20] Canning later declared to Channel 4 News that the fact that 'issues like gay marriage and abortion rights are a devolved matter is completely out of order'.[21] As a direct follow-on from McKee's murder, the Rainbow Project in Northern Ireland organised a rally for marriage equality through Belfast city on 18 May 2019. Canning agreed to address gathered crowds at the rally outside Belfast City Hall, poignantly the same place that the first civil partnership in the United Kingdom was held in 2005.

The murder of Lyra McKee brought the issue of marriage equality back under the spotlight in Northern Ireland. In July 2019, a group of MPs from across party lines introduced a bill which would see marriage extended to same-sex couples in the North of Ireland within three months, unless the devolved government at Stormont re-established in that time. The amendment was supported by Justine Greening, former Education and Equalities Minister, along with Green MP Caroline Lucas, the Labour Party's Owen Smith, Liberal Democrat Layla Moran and Tory MP Nick Herbert.

On 9 July, MPs voted on the call to extend marriage to same-sex couples at Westminster, if the Northern Ireland Assembly were not restored within the stated three-month timeframe. There was an overwhelming call to pass marriage equality, with 383 MPs voting in favour, against only 73 in opposition. Fergal McFerran, who knew Ms McKee, said 'it is incredibly poignant that today is a day that I'm sure Lyra and her partner Sara would have been looking forward to and it's incredibly sad that she's not here to see the progress that has been made, but I think the LGBT community as a whole take inspiration from her every day'.[22] Westminster passed the Northern Ireland Executive Formation Act in October 2019 legislating to extend civil marriage to same-sex couples. This law was enacted on 13 January 2020; Robyn Peoples and Sharni Edwards became the first same sex couple to marry in Northern Ireland on 11 February 2020.

## Notes

1  All marriage figures taken from the Central Statistics Office website, available at: www.cso.ie/en/statistics/birthsdeathsandmarriages/marriages civilpartnerships/ (accessed 26 July 2018).
2  Department of Health, 'Children and Family Relationships (Amendment) Bill 2018 approved by the Houses of the Oireachtas', press release (18 July 2018), available at: https://health.gov.ie/blog/press-release/children-and-family-relationships-amendment-bill-2018-app roved-by-the-houses-of-the-oireachtas/ (accessed 6 September 2019).
3  Baker, 'Same-sex parents'.
4  Ruth Coppinger, 'Children and Family Relationships (Amendment) Bill 2018: Committee and remaining stages', *Dáil Éireann Debate* (11 July 2018).
5  Department of Health, 'Children and Family Relationships (Amendment) Bill 2018 approved by the Houses of the Oireachtas'.

6 Sam McBride, 'Assembly members vote to block gay marriage', *News Letter* (26 June 2013).

7 Owen Bowcott, 'Gay marriage cake row reaches UK's supreme court in Belfast', *Guardian* (1 May 2018).

8 Owen Bowcott, 'UK supreme court backs bakery that refused to make gay marriage cake', *Guardian* (10 October 2018).

9 Ibid.

10 Cromie, 'Gay marriage'.

11 Henry McDonald, 'Couples challenge Northern Ireland's gay marriage ban in court', *Guardian* (24 June 2015).

12 Caroline Mortimer, 'Northern Ireland same-sex marriage vote vetoed by DUP', *Independent UK* (2 November 2015).

13 Claire Smyth, 'Stormont's petition of concern used 115 times in five years', *The Detail* (29 September 2016).

14 Ian McKellan, 'Sir Ian McKellan writes in support of same sex marriage in Northern Ireland', *Attitude* (2 November 2015).

15 Nick Duffy, 'Northern Ireland: couple launch legal bid for same-sex marriage recognition', *Pink News* (15 January 2015).

16 'Judge dismisses Northern Ireland same-sex marriage cases', *BBC News* (17 August 2017), available at: www.bbc.com/news/uk-northern-ireland-40954619 (accessed 31 July 2018).

17 'McDonald: Westminster should break same-sex marriage impasse', *Evening Telegraph* (30 July 2018).

18 An agreement between the British-based National Union of Students (NUS) and the Union of Students in Ireland (USI) to jointly organise and encourage unison across sectarian divides in Northern Ireland.

19 Gareth Cross, 'Lyra McKee was planning to propose to partner Sara next month, funeral told', *Belfast Telegraph* (24 April 2019).

20 Matta Busby, 'Lyra McKee's partner pleads for same-sex marriage in Northern Ireland', *Guardian* (8 May 2019).

21 Ibid.

22 David Young, 'Marriage equality campaigners celebrate "historic day" for Northern Ireland', *Irish Times* (9 July 2019).

# Appendix 1

A message on the marriage referendum: 'Care for the covenant of marriage' by Archbishop Eamon Martin.

To interfere with the definition of marriage is not a simple or a trivial matter – Archbishop Martin

On 22 May 2015 a referendum will take place in the Republic of Ireland on the introduction of same-sex marriage. Archbishop Eamon Martin, Archbishop of Armagh and Primate of All Ireland said in a statement:

In recent weeks and months I have received many letters and messages asking me, as a Bishop, to explain clearly the Church's teaching on marriage in the context of the forthcoming referendum. The Irish bishops have already said that we cannot support an amendment to the Constitution which redefines marriage and effectively places the union of two men, or two women, on a par with the marriage relationship between a husband and wife which is open to the procreation of children.

The Church's vision for marriage and the family is based on faith and reason and it is shared by many people of all faith traditions and none. Since time immemorial, Church and State have recognised marriage to be of fundamental importance for children, mothers and fathers, and society. To interfere with the definition of marriage is not a simple or a trivial matter.

The teaching of the Catholic Church on the issue of same-sex unions was reiterated at the Extraordinary Synod on the Family in Rome, 2014: 'There are absolutely no grounds for considering homosexual unions to be in any way similar or even remotely analogous to God's plan for marriage and family' (Synod Report n55). At the same time, the Church emphasises that gay people ought always to be treated with respect and sensitivity.

## The 'dignity of difference' between male and female

As people of faith, we believe that the union of a man and a woman in marriage, open to the procreation of children, is a gift from God who created us 'male and female'. But we are also people of reason, who hold to the truth about human sexuality, grounded in the natural law, that the relationship between a man and a woman is unique.

How have we got ourselves into the situation that when people stand up to guard the dignity of difference between a man and woman, and speak for the traditional definition of marriage, they are often portrayed as being against freedom, or against equality? How is it that many people won't even raise these issues in their families and workplaces for fear of being ridiculed or condemned as homophobic? Could we not expect at least some of our legislators to engage in public discussion on both sides of this debate?

Until now, Ireland has accepted that it is in the best interests of children and of society to promote and protect the model of children being born and raised in a family with their biological parents. The proposed amendment to the Constitution will remove the unique and privileged status in society for the marriage between a man and a woman. It is worth noting what Pope Francis has said recently: 'When the stable and fruitful covenant between a man and a woman is devalued by society, it is a loss for everyone, especially the young' (General Audience 22nd April 2015).

### Care for the covenant of marriage – Pope Francis

We read in the Book of Genesis that from the beginning, God created human beings in His own image – 'male and female' – and commissioned them to 'be fruitful'. Marriage is willed by God, and instituted and sanctified by God, to be the way in which God's work of creation continues in the world. The gift of life, which flows from the intimate union of a man and woman in marriage, is a gift from God Himself.

Catholics give marriage the dignity of a 'sacrament' because it mirrors the mystery of God's love for humans and of Christ's love for His Church. Pope St John Paul II, who is remembered as the 'Pope of the Family' described marriage as the 'primordial sacrament' – in the sense that it is the original and most ancient sacrament which belongs to creation itself. In April, Pope Francis reminded us that marriage is a 'noble vocation' and he urged all of us to care for the 'covenant' of marriage between man and woman.

The gift of life, which flows from the intimate union of a man and woman in marriage, is a gift from God Himself.

### A misunderstanding of 'equality'

What makes marriage unique among other types of relationship is the distinctiveness of the union between a man and a woman which is open to life. To remove this specific difference is not, as some would argue, a development or evolution of our understanding of marriage; it is, rather, a very definite break with human history and with the natural institution of marriage. We end up using the term 'marriage' for something that it is not. Many of the arguments being made for the proposed amendment appear to be based on a misunderstanding of 'equality'. It is a fact of nature that same-sex unions are fundamentally and objectively different from the complementary sexual union of a woman and a man which is, of itself, naturally open to life.

During the current debate we are conscious of same-sex partners who love each other and wish to share their life together. 'Marriage' is about much more than a loving relationship between consenting adults. Marriage has another essential element – the openness to children who are born of the love and sexual relationship of their mother and father. This is why, as Article 41:3:1 of the Constitution puts it: 'The State pledges itself to guard with special care the institution of Marriage, on which the Family is founded, and to protect it against attack.' The State encourages and favours the marriage of a man and a woman, open to children, because it is for the common good. It not only satisfies individual love and needs, but it also ensures the future of society and forms the ideal environment for the development of children.

We know, of course, that, as Pope Francis put it recently: 'A perfect family does not exist'. Many families experience great trials, and struggle with wounded relationships and disappointments. Tensions and loneliness can build up within the home. The marriage relationship does not always 'work out' as hoped for. Sadly, and despite their best intentions, many married couples separate, often for the good of their children and for their own well-being. We also know that many parents are generously and successfully raising children on their own, and many others are giving great love and joy to children through adoption and fostering. This does not mean, however, that we should not continue to hold up the example of a faithful, life-long and committed marriage relationship between a man and a woman as something beautiful and special. Society should do everything in its power to support and encourage this unique union so that as many children as possible can have a father and a mother who live together in a relationship marked by stability and love.

What makes marriage unique among other types of relationship is the distinctiveness of the union between a man and a woman which is open to life.

### Freedom of conscience

Some commentators have said that 'sacramental' or 'religious' marriage is not affected by the proposed amendment. It is important to remember that religious freedom means much more than simply the freedom to worship or have ceremonies of a particular type. Freedom of religion is linked very closely to freedom of conscience and freedom to express publicly our values and beliefs in daily life.

If society adopts and imposes a 'new orthodoxy' of 'gender-neutral' marriage, being defined simply as a union between any two persons – including a man and a man, or a woman and [a] woman – then it will become increasingly difficult to speak or teach in public about marriage as being between a man and a woman. Will there be lawsuits against individuals and groups who do not share this vision? What will we be expected to teach children in school about marriage or about homosexual acts? Will those who continue to sincerely believe that marriage is between a man and a woman be forced to act against their faith and conscience?

Freedom of religion is linked very closely to freedom of conscience and freedom to express publicly our values and beliefs in daily life.

### *Reflect and pray before you vote*

I encourage everyone to reflect and pray carefully about these issues before voting on 22 May. It is very important to vote. Do not be afraid to speak up courageously for the union of a man and a woman in marriage.

Pope Francis reminds us: 'While a noble vocation, marriage is not an easy one: it must constantly be strengthened by a living relationship with the Lord through prayer: mornings and evenings, at meals, in the recitation of the Rosary, and above all through the Sunday Eucharist.'

I invite you, especially in May, the month of Mary, to pray the Rosary for all the families of Ireland, remembering those who are especially in need of prayer at this time. May our families be models of faith, love and generous service.

### *Prayer to the Holy Family*

Jesus, Mary and Joseph, in you we contemplate the splendour of true love, to you we turn with trust.

Holy Family of Nazareth, grant that our families too may be places of communion and prayer, authentic schools of the Gospel and small domestic Churches.

Holy Family of Nazareth, may families never again experience violence, rejection and division: may all who have been hurt or scandalised find ready comfort and healing.

Holy Family of Nazareth, may the approaching Synod of Bishops make us once more mindful of the sacredness and inviolability of the family, and its beauty in God's plan.

Jesus, Mary and Joseph, graciously hear our prayer.
Amen.

Source: Irish Catholic Media Office, released 2 May 2015.

# Appendix 2

Ursula Halligan, 'Referendum led me to tell truth about myself' – *Irish Times* (15 May 2015)

Our lives begin to end the day we become silent about things that matter – Martin Luther King

I was a good Catholic girl, growing up in 1970s Ireland where homosexuality was an evil perversion. It was never openly talked about but I knew it was the worst thing on the face of the earth.

So when I fell in love with a girl in my class in school, I was terrified. Rummaging around in the attic a few weeks ago, an old diary brought me right back to December 20th, 1977.

"These past few months must have been the darkest and gloomiest I have ever experienced in my entire life," my 17-year-old self wrote.

"There have been times when I have even thought about death, of escaping from this world, of sleeping untouched by no-one forever. I have been so depressed, so sad and so confused. There seems to be no one I can turn to, not even God. I've poured out my emotions, my innermost thoughts to him and get no relief or so-called spiritual grace. At times I feel I am talking to nothing, that no God exists. I've never felt like this before, so empty, so meaningless, so utterly, utterly miserable."

Because of my upbringing, I was revolted at the thought that I was in love with a member of my own sex. This contradiction within me nearly drove me crazy. These two strands of thought jostled within me pulling me in opposite directions.

## Plagued with fear

I loved a girl and I knew that wasn't right; my mind was constantly plagued with the fear that I was a lesbian. I hated myself. I felt useless and worthless and very small and stupid. I had one option, and only one option. I would be "normal", and that meant locking myself in the closet and throwing away the key.

I played the dating game. I feigned interest in men. I invented boyfriends. I listened silently to snide remarks about homosexuals. Tried to smile at mimicry of stereotypical gay behaviour.

In the 1970s, homophobia was rampant and uninhibited. Political correctness had yet to arrive. Homosexuals were faggots, queers, poofs, freaks, deviants, unclean, unnatural, mentally ill, second class and defective humans. They were society's defects. Biological errors. They were other people. I couldn't possibly be one of them.

Over the years I watched each of my siblings date, party, get engaged, get married and take for granted all the joys and privileges of their State-acknowledged relationship.

My coping strategy was to pour myself into my studies and later into my work. I didn't socialise much because I had this horrible secret that must never come out. It was a strategy that worked until I'd fall in love again with a woman and the whole emotional roller-coaster of bliss, pain, withdrawal and denial resumed. It was a pattern that would repeat itself over the years.

And never once did I openly express my feelings. I suppressed everything and buried myself in books or work. I was careful how I talked and behaved. Nothing was allowed slip. I never knew what it was like to live spontaneously, to go with the flow, to trust my instincts … I certainly couldn't trust my instincts.

## Repressing my humanity

For years I told no one because I couldn't even tell myself. It was a place I didn't want to go. It was too scary; too shameful. I couldn't cope with it. I buried it.

Emotionally, I have been in a prison since the age of 17; a prison where I lived a half-life, repressing an essential part of my humanity, the expression of my deepest self; my instinct to love.

It's a part that heterosexual people take for granted, like breathing air. The world is custom-tailored for them. At every turn society assumes and confirms heterosexuality as the norm. This culminates in marriage when the happy couple is showered with an outpouring of overwhelming social approval.

For me, there was no first kiss; no engagement party; no wedding. And up until a short time ago no hope of any of these things. Now, at the age of 54, in a (hopefully) different Ireland, I wish I had broken out of my prison cell a long time ago. I feel a sense of loss and sadness for precious time spent wasted in fear and isolation.

Homophobia was so deeply embedded in my soul, I resisted facing the truth about myself, preferring to live in the safety of my prison. In the privacy of my head, I had become a roaring, self-loathing homophobe, resigned to going to my grave with my shameful secret. And I might well have done that if the referendum hadn't come along.

Now, I can't quite believe the pace of change that's sweeping across the globe in support of gay marriage. I never thought I'd see the day that a Government Minister would come out as gay and encounter almost nothing but praise for his bravery. But that day did come, and the work done down the decades by people like David Norris, Katherine Zappone, Ann-Louise Gilligan and Colm O'Gorman made me realise that possibilities existed that I'd never believed would ever exist.

I told a friend and the world didn't end. I told my mother, and the world didn't end.

Then I realised that I could leave the prison completely or stay in the social equivalent of an open prison. The second option would mean telling a handful of people but essentially go on as before, silently colluding with the prejudices that still find expression in casual social moments.

It's the easier of the two options, particularly for those close to me. Because those who love you can cope with you coming out, but they're wary of you "making an issue" of it.

### Game-changer

The game-changer was the marriage equality referendum. It pointed me toward the first option: telling the truth to anyone who cares. And I knew if I was going to tell the truth, I had to tell the whole truth and reveal my backing for a Yes vote. For me, the two are intrinsically linked.

That means TV3 taking me off referendum coverage. The rules say they must, and when I told them my situation, they reorganised their coverage in half a day.

Twenty years ago or 30 years ago, it would have taken more courage than I had to tell the truth. Today, it's still difficult but it can be done with hope – hope that most people in modern Ireland embrace diversity and would understand that I'm trying to be helpful to other gay people leading small, frightened, incomplete lives. If my story helps even one 17-year-old school girl, struggling with her sexuality, it will have been worth it.

As a person of faith and a Catholic, I believe a Yes vote is the most Christian thing to do. I believe the glory of God is the human being fully alive and that this includes people who are gay.

If Ireland votes Yes, it will be about much more than marriage. It will end institutional homophobia. It will say to gay people that they belong, that it's safe to surface and live fully human, loving lives. If it's true that 10 per cent of any population are gay, then there could be 400,000 gay people out there; many of them still living in emotional prisons. Any of them could be your son, daughter, brother, sister, mother, father or best friend. Set them free. Allow them live full lives.

# Select bibliography

## General

Ahern, Bertie, Trevor Sargent and Mary Harney, *Programme for Government 2007–2012*, Dublin, June 2007.

Allain, Jean and Siobhán Mullally (eds), *The Irish Yearbook of International Law, Volume 3*, Oxford, 2008.

Bacik, Ivana and Mary Rogan (eds), *Legal Cases that Changed Ireland*, Dublin, 2016.

Bird, Charlie, *One Day in May: Real lives, true stories*, Dublin, 2016.

Centre for Evaluation Innovation, *Civil Partnership and Ireland: How a minority advocacy group achieved a majority*, case study of the Gay and Lesbian Equality Network (November 2012).

Colley, Anne, *Options Paper presented by the Working Group on Domestic Partnership* (November 2006).

Convention on the Constitution, *Third Report of the Convention on the Constitution: Amending the Constitution to provide for same-sex marriage* (June 2013), available at: www.constitution.ie (accessed 24 July 2017).

Cook, Barbary and Rebecca Subar, *Catalysing LGBT Equality and Visibility in Ireland: A review of LGBT cluster grants, 2004–2013* (2014).

Coppinger, Ruth, 'Children and Family Relationships (Amendment) Bill 2018: Committee and remaining stages', *Dáil Éireann Debate* (11 July 2018).

Dáil Éireann, 'Civil Unions Bill 2006: Second stage', *Dáil Éireann Debate*, Vol. 631, No. 6 (20 February 2007).

Dáil Éireann, 'Civil Unions Bill 2006: Restoration to order paper', *Dáil Éireann Debate*, Vol. 640, No. 4 (31 October 2007).

Dáil Éireann, 'Private Members' Business – Civil Unions Bill 2006: Restoration to order paper (resumed)', *Dáil Éireann Debate*, Vol. 640, No. 51 (1 November 2007).

Dáil Éireann, 'Third Report of the Constitutional Convention – Same-Sex Marriage: Statements', *Dáil Éireann Debate*, Vol. 825, No. 1 (17 December 2013).

Dáil Éireann, 'RTÉ Compensation Payment', *Dáil Éireann Debate*, Vol. 829, No. 3 (6 February 2014).

Dáil Éireann, 'Broadcasting (Amendment) Bill 2014: First stage', *Parliamentary Debates: Dáil Éireann*, Vol. 833, No. 2 (5 March 2014).

Dáil Éireann, 'Broadcasting (Amendment) Bill 2014: Second stage [Private Members]', *Parliamentary Debates: Dáil Éireann*, Vol. 837, No. 4 (11 April 2014).

Department of Justice and Equality, 'Publication of Civil Partnership Bill', press release (24 June 2008).

Department of Justice and Equality, 'Children and Family Relationships Bill 2013: Briefing note' (5 November 2013).

Department of the Taoiseach, *Programme for Government 2011* (7 June 2011).

Donnelly, Deputy Stephen S., 'Broadcasting (Amendment) Bill 2014: First stage', *Dáil Éireann Debate*, Vol. 833, No. 2 (5 March 2014).

Dwyer, Craig (ed.), *Gay Law Reform Debates 1993: Dáil and Seanad*, Dublin, 2013.

Elkink, Johan A., David M. Farrell, Theresa Reidy and Jane Suiter, 'Understanding the 2015 Marriage Referendum in Ireland: Context, campaign, and conservative Ireland', *Irish Political Studies*, 32:3 (2017), 361–81.

Equality Authority, *Annual Report 2003*, Dublin, 2004.

Fagan, Paula, *Missing Pieces: A comparison of the rights and responsibilities gained from civil partnership compared to the rights and responsibilities gained through civil marriage in Ireland*, Dublin, 2011.

Fianna Fáil, *Real Plan, Better Future*, Fianna Fáil Manifesto (2011).

Fine Gael, *Fine Gael Manifesto* (2011).

Gately, Susan, 'RTÉ apologises for "homophobic" accusations on Saturday show' (28 January 2014), available at: www.catholicireland.net/rte-apologises-homophobic-accusations-saturday-show/ (accessed 11 April 2017).

Gilligan, Ann Louise and Katherine Zappone, *Our Lives Out Loud: In pursuit of justice and equality*, Dublin, 2008.

Gilmore, Éamon, *Inside the Room: The untold story of Ireland's crisis government*, Dublin, 2016.

GLEN, *Dáil and Seanad Debates on Decriminalisation of Homosexuality* (June 1993).

GLEN, *Diversity Powering Success: The Building Sustainable Change Programme* (April 2006).

Glynn, Irial with Tomás and Piaras Mac Éinrí, *The Re-emergence of Emigration from Ireland: New trends in an old story*, Washington DC, 2015.

Green Party, *Playing to Our Strengths*, Green Party Manifesto (2011).

Healy, Gráinne, 'Change the law first, not the Constitution says Marriage Equality', press release, Marriage Equality (17 February 2008).

Healy, Gráinne, 'We deserve equality: Marriage Equality Co-chair tells launch audience', press release, Marriage Equality (19 February 2008).

Healy, Gráinne, Brian Sheehan and Noel Whelan, *Ireland Says Yes: The inside story of how the vote for marriage equality was won*, Dublin, 2016.

Healy, Gráinne (ed.), *Crossing the Threshold: The story of the marriage equality movement*, Dublin, 2017.

Howlin, Brendan, 'Civil Partnership Bill falls short of Government commitment on equality', available at: www.labour.ie (accessed 26 June 2009).

ICCL Working Group on Partnership Rights and Family Diversity, *Equality for All Families*, Dublin, 2006.

Irish Human Rights Commission, *Discussion Document on the Scheme of the Civil Partnership Bill* (December 2008).

Isbell, Matthew, 'The numbers behind Ireland's historic vote on same-sex marriage', *MCI Maps* (26 May 2015), available at: http://mcimaps.com/the-numbers-behind-irelands-historic-vote-on-same-sex-marriage/ (accessed 11 July 2018).

Kelly, Brendan, *Hearing Voices: The history of psychiatry in Ireland*, Dublin, 2016.

Labour Party, *The Fair Society*, Labour Party Manifesto, 2007.

Labour Party, *One Ireland: Jobs, reform, fairness*, Labour Party Manifesto (2011).

Lacey, Brian, *Terrible Queer Creatures*, Dublin, 2008.

Law Reform Commission, *Legal Aspects of Family Relationships* (LRC 101–2010).

LGBT Network Service Providers, *LGBT Network News: Fortnightly e-newsletter*, Issue 20 (19 April 2006).

Marriage Equality, 'New report reveals 169 differences between civil marriage and civil partnership', press release (4 October 2011).

Martin, archbishop Eamon, *Care for the Covenant of Marriage*, Irish Catholic Media Office (2 May 2015).

Masci, David, Elizabeth Sciupac and Michael Lipka, *Gay Marriage around the World*, Washington DC, 2014.

McManus, Sally, *Sexual Orientation Research Phase 1: A review of methodological approaches*, Edinburgh, 2003.

Mullally, Una, *In the Name of Love: The movement for marriage equality in Ireland – an oral history*, Dublin, 2014.

Murphy, Yvonne, 'The marriage equality referendum 2015', *Irish Political Studies*, 31:2 (2016), 315–30.

Ní Bhroin, Feargha, *Feminism and the Same-Sex Marriage Debate* (April 2009).

O'Carroll, Íde and Finbar McDonnell, *Marriage Equality: Case study, final version* (September 2010).

O'Gorman, Colm, 'Family in No poster says Yes to marriage equality in Ireland', Amnesty International Ireland (7 May 2015), available at: www. amnesty.org/en/latest/news/2015/05/family-in-no-poster-says-yes-to-marriage-equality-in-ireland/ (accessed 2 July 2018).

Ó Snodaigh, Aengus, 'Government must do better than Civil Partnership Bill' (24 June 2008), available at: www.sinnfein.ie/contents/13050 (accessed 6 July 2008).

Parker, Susan, *The Path to Marriage Equality in Ireland: A case study*, 2017, available at: www.atlanticphilanthropies.org/wp-content/uploads/2018/01/Marriage_Equality_Case_Study.pdf (accessed 1 January 2019).

Pillinger, Jane, *Making the Case for Marriage Equality in Ireland: Marriage Equality position paper* (February 2008).

Power, Senator Averil, 'Order of Business', *Seanad Éireann Debate* (30 January 2014).

Power, Averil, 'Statement by Senator Averil Power on resigning from Fianna Fáil' (25 May 2015), available at: https://static.rasset.ie/documents/news/statement-by-senator-averil-power-on-resigning-from-fianna-fail. pdf (accessed 13 July 2018).

Referendum Commission, *Report on the Referendums on Marriage and on the Age of Presidential Candidates* (October 2015).

Republic of Ireland, *Bunreacht Na hÉireann, Constitution of Ireland*, Dublin, [1937] 2012.

Seanad Éireann, 'Civil Partnership Bill 2004: Second stage, Seanad Éireann', *Parliamentary Debates*, Vol. 179, No. 8 (16 February 2005).

Shanahan, Niall, 'YES Equality, voter registration campaign launch', *Impact Member's e-bulletin* (7 November 2014), available at: http://impacttrade-union.newsweaver.com/newsletter/1b0q0v5nqab (accessed 26 April 2017).

Sheehan, Brian, *GLEN Submission to the Joint Oireachtas Committee on Justice, Defence and Equality on the Heads of the Children and Family Relationships Bill* (February 2014).

Sinn Féin, *There is a Better Way*, Sinn Féin General Election Manifesto (2011).

SIPTU, 'Yes Equality campaign takes to the road', SIPTU news release (22 April 2015), available at: www.siptu.ie/media/newsarchive2015/fullstory_19039_en.html (accessed 6 July 2018).

Solomon, Marc, *Winning Marriage: The inside story of how same-sex couples took on the politicians and pundits—and won*, New England, 2014.

Tiernan, Sonja, 'Countess Markievicz and Eva Gore-Booth', in Eugenio Biagini and Daniel Mulhall (eds), *The Shaping of Modern Ireland: A centenary assessment*, Dublin, 2016, pp. 185–97.

Treacy, Patrick SC, Shane Murphy SC and William Binchy, 'Senior lawyers urge no vote in marriage referendum', Iona Institute for Religion and Society website (15 May 2015), available at: https://ionainstitute.ie/senior-lawyers-urge-no-vote-in-marriage-referendum/ (accessed 10 July 2018).

Walsh, Fintan, *Queer Performance and Contemporary Ireland: Dissent and disorientation*, London, 2016.

Walsh, Judy, Catherine Conlon, Barry Fitzpatrick and Ulf Hansson, *Enabling Lesbian, Gay and Bisexual Individuals to Access Their Rights under Equality Law: A Report Prepared for the Equality Commission for Northern Ireland and The Equality Authority* (November 2007).

Wolfenden, John, *Report on the Committee on Homosexual Offences and Prostitution*, London, 1957.

Zappone, Katherine, 'Civil Law (Miscellaneous Provisions) Bill 2011: Report stage', *Seanad Éireann Debate*, Vol. 209, No. 5 (7 July 2011).

Zappone, Katherine, 'In pursuit of marriage equality in Ireland: A narrative and theoretical reflection', *Equal Rights Review*, 10 (2013), 111–22.

Zappone, Katherine, *Submission to the Constitutional Convention on Marriage for Same-Sex Couples* (11 March 2013).

Zappone, Katherine, 'Free Speech, Homophobia and Public Service Role of State Broadcaster: Motion [Private Members]', *Parliamentary Debates: Seanad Éireann*, Vol. 229, No. 13 (18 February 2014).

## Newspapers and magazines

Agnew, Paddy, 'Marriage referendum a "defeat for humanity" – does the Vatican just not get it?', *Irish Times* (30 May 2015).

Arnold, Tom, 'Inside the convention on the constitution', *Irish Times* (1 April 2014).

Baker, Noel, 'Same-sex parents "in legal quagmire"', *Irish Examiner* (19 May 2016).

Barry, Aoife, 'RTÉ apologises for "distress" caused by Saturday Night Show guest's comments', *The Journal* (26 January 2014).

Beesley, Arthur, 'A yes vote is good for business', *Irish Times* (1 May 2015).

Belfast Telegraph Digital, 'Dublin priest receives standing ovation after saying he is gay during mass', *Belfast Telegraph* (9 January 2015), available at: www.belfasttelegraph.co.uk/news/republic-of-ireland/dublin-priest-receives-standing-ovation-after-saying-he-is-gay-during-mass-30894 931.html (accessed 11 April 2017).

Bliss, Panti (Rory O'Neill), 'A Noble Call at the Abbey Theatre', full transcript in Shaun Connolly, 'Buttimer and Panti drown out empty rhetoric in homophobia debate', *Irish Examiner* (8 February 2014).

Bowcott, Owen, 'Gay marriage cake row reaches UK's supreme court in Belfast', *Guardian* (1 May 2018).

Bowcott, Owen, 'UK supreme court backs bakery that refused to make gay marriage cake', *Guardian* (10 October 2018).

Britto, Fr John, 'Full sermon of Fr. John Britto on same sex marriage', *Donegal Daily* (20 March 2015).

Busby, Matta, 'Lyra McKee's partner pleads for same-sex marriage in Northern Ireland', *Guardian* (8 May 2019).

Carbery, Genevieve, 'Dublin Pride celebrations soured by anger over Civil Partnership Bill', *Irish Times* (29 June 2009).

Carr, Aoife, 'Group calls for equal marriage rights', *Irish Times* (4 October 2011).

Carroll, Steven, 'Call for full equality by same-sex couple', *Irish Times* (19 February 2008).

Carroll, Steven, 'Greens seek support for same-sex marriage', *Irish Times* (19 February 2008).

Carty, Ed and Noel Baker, 'Ban Ki-moon praises Ireland on marriage equality vote', *Irish Examiner* (24 May 2015).

Charlton, Denise and Paula Fagan, 'Time to open civil marriage to lesbian and gay couples', *Irish Times* (25 February 2008).

Chayter, Rod, 'Travel pass for gay pensioner's lover', *The Mirror* (26 September 2003).

Collins, Stephen, 'Same-sex couples to get legal recognition next year', *Irish Times* (1 November 2007).

Collins, Stephen, 'Gay adoption law due before same-sex marriage referendum', *Irish Times* (21 January 2015).

Courtney, Joan and Frances Byrne, 'Debate on same-sex marriage', *Irish Times* (28 February 2008).

Coyne, Ellen, 'Repeal leaders named icons for "transforming view of Ireland"', *The Times* (18 April 2019).

Cromie, Claire, 'Gay marriage now has overwhelming support in Northern Ireland – poll', *Belfast Telegraph* (6 July 2015).

Crosbie, Tom, 'Civil Partnership Bill to fall short of groups' demands', *Irish Examiner* (4 April 2008).

Cross, Gareth, 'Lyra McKee was planning to propose to partner Sara next month, funeral told', *Belfast Telegraph* (24 April 2019).

Curran, Tom, 'As a man of faith and a proud Dad to a gay son, I urge all Catholics to do the right thing – and vote yes', *Irish Independent* (9 May 2015).

D'Arcy, Ciaran, 'Leo Varadkar: "I am a gay man," Minister says', *Irish Times* (18 January 2015).

de Burca, Demelza, '58% back gay marriage', *Irish Daily Mirror* (1 April 2008).

Duffy, Nick, 'Northern Ireland: couple launch legal bid for same-sex marriage recognition', *Pink News* (15 January 2015).

Duffy, Rónán, '"A thumping majority" – High Court rejects two legal challenges to marriage referendum', *The Journal* (5 June 2015).

Dugan, Emily, 'Ireland's same-sex marriage vote: as date looms, the Irish ask – how would God vote?', *Independent UK* (20 May 2015).

Feder, J. Lester, 'There is a battle going on within the Irish Catholic Church at the moment', *BuzzFeed News*, 18 May 2015, available at: www.buzz feednews.com/article/lesterfeder/priests-defy-bishops-to-support-mar riage-equality-in-ireland (accessed 6 September 2019).

Ferriter, Diarmaid, 'Recapturing relevance a huge challenge for FF', *Irish Times* (1 March 2011).

Finn, Christina, 'Why did Roscommon-South Leitrim vote No?', *The Journal* (24 May 2015).

Gartland, Fiona, 'Marriage equality is a human right, says Law Society', *Irish Times* (7 May 2015).

Geen, Jessica, 'Video: Irish gay marriage ad becomes a surprise internet hit', *Pink News* (4 September 2009).

Grew, Tony, 'Gay rights group pays tribute to Bertie Ahern', *Pink News* (4 April 2008), available at: www.pinknews.co.uk/2008/04/04/gay-rights-group-pays-tribute-to-bertie-ahern/ (accessed 16 August 2018).

Griffin, Dan, 'The counts – Ireland votes Yes', *Irish Times* (23 May 2015).

Halligan, Ursula, 'Referendum led me to tell the truth about myself', *Irish Times* (15 May 2015).

Hand, Lise, 'Leo Varadkar calls for a Yes vote in marriage equality referendum', *Irish Independent* (5 May 2015).

Hayden, Esther, '"Walk-out" during mass at cathedral over letter from bishop', *Irish Independent* (16 May 2015).

Healy, Alison, 'Diarmuid Martin: Catholic Church needs reality check', *Irish Times* (23 May 2015).

Healy, Catherine, 'Why young voters mobilised for same sex marriage', *Irish Times* (23 May 2015).

Hennessy, Mark, 'FF Senator leads move to deny gay couples right to register', *Irish Times* (27 June 2008).

Hicks, George, 'Yes Equality campaign launched in Dublin', *Pink News*
(9 March 2015).

Holland, Kitty, 'Children's charities call for a Yes in same-sex marriage vote',
*Irish Times* (29 April 2015).

Independent.ie reporter, 'Cork Fine Gael deputy Jerry Buttimer comes out
saying: I'm a TD who just happens to be gay', *Irish Independent* (30 April
2012), available at: www.independent.ie/irish-news/cork-fine-gael-dep
uty-jerry-buttimer-comes-out-saying-im-a-td-who-just-happens-to-
be-gay-26848351.html (accessed 11 July 2018).

Ingle, Róisín, 'Families come out for gay marriage', *Irish Times* (16 February
2008).

Kearns, David, 'Families hit out over "No" campaign poster criticising surrogacy', *Irish Independent* (23 April 2015).

Kearns, David, 'Ireland's first same sex marriage takes place in Tipperary',
*Irish Independent* (17 November 2015).

Kirchgaessner, Stephanie, 'Vatican says Ireland gay marriage vote is "defeat
for humanity"', *Guardian* (26 May 2015).

Mac Cormaic, Ruadhan, 'Constitutional convention backs extension
of marriage rights to same-sex couples', *Irish Times* (15 April
2013).

McBride, Sam, 'Assembly members vote to block gay marriage', *News Letter*
(26 June 2013).

McDonald, Henry, 'Couples challenge Northern Ireland's gay marriage ban
in court', *Guardian* (24 June 2015).

McGarry, Patsy, 'Fr Iggy O'Donovan calls for Yes vote in marriage referendum', *Irish Times* (10 March 2015).

McKellan, Ian, 'Sir Ian McKellan writes in support of same sex marriage in
Northern Ireland', *Attitude* (2 November 2015).

McTeirnan, Anthea, 'On the road to somewhere: the bus driver's tale', *Irish
Times* (20 May 2015).

Meneely, Gary, 'Priest comes out at mass', *Irish Sun* (6 January 2015).

Mills, Keith, 'Why I'll be voting "No" to same-sex marriage, even though
I'm gay', *Irish Independent* (1 February 2015).

Minihan, Mary, 'Mothers and Fathers Matter launches No referendum
campaign', *Irish Times* (17 April 2015).

Mortimer, Caroline, 'Northern Ireland same-sex marriage vote vetoed by
DUP', *Independent UK* (2 November 2015).

Neville, Sarah, 'Half of us say gays should be allowed to get married', *Irish
Independent* (1 April 2008).

Nianias, Helen, 'Archbishop of Dublin Diarmuid Martin says yes vote for gay marriage shows weakening Catholic church in Ireland', *Independent* (24 May 2015).

O'Brien, Carl, 'Improved terms for cohabiting couples proposed', *Irish Times* (23 November 2006).

O'Brien, Carl, 'Lenihan rules out "divisive" referendum on gay marriage', *Irish Times* (5 December 2007).

O'Brien, Carl, 'Same-sex unions to get many benefits of marriage', *Irish Times* (1 April 2008).

O'Brien, Carl, 'Mixed response to plans for civil unions', *Irish Times* (2 April 2008).

O'Brien, Carl, 'Sr. Stan to vote in favour of same sex marriage', *Irish Times* (11 May 2015).

O'Brien, David, 'Ireland is warming to gay marriage', *Irish Daily Star* (1 April 2008).

O'Carroll, Sinead, 'Part of *The Saturday Night Show* removed from RTÉ Player over "legal issues"', *The Journal* (15 January 2014).

O'Connor, Niall and John Downing, 'Fianna Fáil senator Jim Walsh resigns from party over his opposition to Children and Family Relationship Bill', *Irish Independent* (26 March 2015).

O'Loughlin, Ann, 'Married lesbians affirm their love while in court', *Irish Independent* (5 October 2006).

O'Loughlin, Ann, 'No difference if children raised by lesbian parents', *Irish Independent* (7 October 2006).

O'Regan, Michael, 'Dáil debates civil unions bill', *Irish Times* (21 January 2010).

O'Regan, Michael, 'Equality group urging Yes in marriage referendum launched', *Irish Times* (9 March 2015).

O'Reilly, Brian, 'Team Panti supporters infiltrate Prime Time audience', *Irish Independent* (12 February 2014).

Phelan, Aishling, 'Rory O'Neill wants personal apology from RTÉ', *Irish Independent* (10 February 2014).

Power, Breda, 'You can't trample over the wedding cake and eat it', *Sunday Times* (5 July 2009).

RED C, 'Same sex marriage opinion poll', *Sunday Business Post* and RTÉ (20 February 2014).

Reilly, Gavin, 'Gilligan and Zappone vow to continue with Supreme Court appeal', *The Journal* (23 October 2011).

Riegel, Ralph and Ryan Nugent, 'Sports stars and women's groups back Yes campaign', *Irish Independent* (6 May 2015).

Robinson, Joanna, 'Read Colin Farrell's impassioned, personal plea for marriage equality in Ireland', *Vanity Fair* (16 November 2014).

Rogers, Stephen, 'Priests' group will not make recommendation in marriage vote', *Irish Examiner* (25 March 2015).

Ryan, Conor, 'Campaign for same-sex marriage takes to the streets', *Irish Examiner* (15 December 2007).

Ryan, Nicky, 'Catholic leaders are out in force arguing against same-sex marriage', *The Journal* (10 May 2015).

Ryan, Órla, 'Church of Ireland won't be campaigning for same-sex marriage vote', *The Journal* (2 February 2015).

Scally, Derek, 'Angela Merkel urged to follow Ireland's lead on same-sex marriage', *Irish Times* (24 May 2015).

Sheehy, Clodagh, 'Anti-gay protesters attack McDowell', *Irish Examiner* (27 May 2006).

Sheridan, Kathy, 'Some Yes campaigners faced subtle, shocking bigotry', *Irish Times* (27 May 2015).

Skibbereen Eagle Online, 'Blessed are the gays, *The Skibbereen Eagle* (11 January 2015), available at: www.skibbereeneagle.ie/uncategorized/blessed-gays (accessed 11 April 2017).

Smyth, Claire, 'Stormont's petition of concern used 115 times in five years', *The Detail* (29 September 2016).

Whelan, Noel, 'Constitutional convention will have its remit severely pruned', *Irish Times* (25 February 2012).

Whelan, Noel, 'Exhausting, draining and life changing: the Yes campaign', *Irish Times* (24 May 2015).

# Index

Lightning Source UK Ltd.
Milton Keynes UK
UKHW021312251021
392810UK00010B/62